To download FREE PDF versions of all the ministry books, on topics including mental health, suicide, sexual abuse, becoming a disciple, the globe deception & intimacy with Jesus, go to the Become Born-again ministry website:

www.becomebornagain.com

All The Ministry Books Available In PDF, Kindle & Paperback

This book is part of an increasing range of books, which are all available in either PDF, Kindle or Paperback format.

To get instant free access to the PDF versions please visit the ministry website:

www.becomebornagain.com/downloads

To purchase the Kindle or Paperback versions please visit Amazon:

https://www.amazon.co.uk/dp/B0CB8S6LX4?binding=paperback

Available Book Titles

- Become A Disciple in 2023 – 77 Pages
- What Is God Saying To His People? Volume 1 – 251 Pages
- What Is God Saying To His People? Volume 2 – 259 Pages
- Sexual Abuse: From Survival To Joy – 239 Pages
- Mental Health: From Prison To Peace – 137 Pages
- The Earth: From Globe Deception to Firmament of Fire – 99 Pages
- Suicide: From Hopeless To Hope – 249 Pages
- Life Behind Bars: From Prison To Purpose – 263 Pages
- Intimacy With Jesus: From Religion To Relationship – 273 Pages

Forthcoming Book Titles In 2023

- Relationships & Marriage: From Ending To Endless
- Single Mums: From Lonely To Loved
- Homeless: From Last To First
- Addict: From Prison To Freedom
- Lust: From Haunted To Holy
- Science: From Research To Revelation
- Space: From Universe To Understanding
- Islam: From Religion To Revelation
- Freemasonry: From Hell To Holy

But he was pierced for our rebellion, crushed for our sins. He was beaten so we could be whole. He was whipped so we could be healed.

Isaiah 53:5

It is the same with my word.
I send it out, and it always produces fruit.
It will accomplish all I want it to,
and it will prosper everywhere I send it.

Isaiah 55:11

RELIGION 6

REVELATION 61

RELATIONSHIP 138

RELIGION

Whether you realise it or not, you may currently be trapped in Religion

What good is it, dear brothers and sisters,
if you say you have faith but
don't show it by your actions?
Can that kind of faith save anyone?

James 2:14

"I know all the things you do, that you are neither hot nor cold. I wish that you were one or the other! But since you are like lukewarm water, neither hot nor cold, I will spit you out of my mouth!

Revelation 3:16

Well then, should we keep on sinning so that God can show us more and more of his wonderful grace? Of course not! Since we have died to sin, how can we continue to live in it? Or have you forgotten that when we were joined with Christ Jesus in baptism, we joined him in his death?

Romans 6:1-3

Remember, it is sin to know what you ought to do and then not do it.

James 4:17

July 25th 2023

One By One This Is What I Am Doing To All My People Trapped In Religion, Says The Lord

My beloved child, I have chosen you and your brothers and sisters to receive my message here, for I am giving you wisdom and revelation of **why and how I am transforming my people from being TRAPPED IN RELIGION to being in a deepening, intimate, LIFE-CHANGING RELATIONSHIP with me.**

Throughout more generations than you can even comprehend, **almost all of my people have been in religion.**

They have not been in a relationship with me.

Since early 2020, I have shown to the whole world that **almost all of my people,** people who say they "believe in God", are trapped in religion.

They **have absolutely no personal relationship with me**, the Lord your God.

They **haven't YET had the revelation, the true revelation, of the depth of my love for them.**

They **haven't YET had the revelation that I surrendered my life on the cross to save THEIR life.**

They **haven't YET had the life-changing revelation that I shed my blood on that cross to atone for all THEIR sins.**

They **haven't YET been willing to truly humble themselves.**

They **haven't YET been willing to deny themselves, pick up THEIR cross DAILY, and follow me.**

They **haven't YET been willing to be hated by the world for being my follower.**

They **haven't YET accepted that without me, without my sacrifice, without my blood, without my Spirit, without my resurrection, they would be a wretched, detestable sinner.**

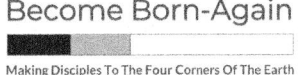

All my people trapped in religion are in SIN.

All my people **trapped** in religion allow MAN TO INFLUENCE AND DICTATE how they live their life.

All my people **trapped** in religion allow the FEAR OF MAN to influence their daily decisions.

All my people **trapped** in religion have NOT been freely giving, as they have freely received.

All my people **trapped** in religion have not begun to experience MY POWER working in and through their lives.

All my people **trapped** in religion have some faith WITHOUT works.

All my people **trapped** in religion are not yet living their life worthy of the calling that they have received.

All my people **trapped** in religion do not yet have a reverent fear of me, the Lord your God.

All my people **trapped** in religion still love things in the world, yet my Word says "Do not love the world, nor the things it offers you."

All my people **trapped** in religion are at best LUKEWARM and my Word tells all my people across the earth that if you are lukewarm, neither cold nor hot, I will vomit you out of my mouth.

All my people **trapped** in religion have NOT YET started being by hands and feet upon the earth.

All my people **trapped** in religion have shown that they are ASHAMED OF THE GOSPEL, for they are not willing to talk to complete strangers to tell them that I love them.

All my people **trapped** in religion have relationships with people but they don't yet have a relationship with me the Lord your God.

My Word says that "Only those with pure hearts and clean hands can climb my holy mountain."

My Words says that "It is a sin to know what you ought to do and then not do it."

My Word says that "I have not given you a spirit of fear, but of power, of love and of a sound mind."

My people **trapped** in religion **have been living with a SPIRIT OF FEAR, and not of power, of love and of a sound mind.**

My people **trapped** in religion **have not been demonstrating and exhibiting the 9 fruit of the Spirit.**

My people **trapped** in religion **have not been demonstrating the gifts of my Spirit, the 9 gifts.**

My beloved child, look around at the nation's!! **Look and be amazed, for I am doing something in your own day, something that you wouldn't even believe even if someone told you about it!** You don't understand what I am doing now but someday you will. Hear this you leaders of the people. Listen all who live in the land. In all your history, **have you ever seen anything like this before?** Tell your children about it in the years to come, and tell your children to tell their children. **Pass the story down from generation to generation.**

My beloved child, one by one, every second of every day, **I AM coming down from heaven mounted on a mighty angelic being to rescue my people from the deep waters.**

One by one **I AM taking my people, men, women, teenagers and children, OUT OF RELIGION and into a personal intimate relationship with me.**

One by one, **I AM giving my people the eyes to see and ears to hear.**

One by one, **I AM lifting the veil.**

One by one, **the scales are falling from their eyes.**

One by one, **I AM destroying all religious spirits.**

One by one, **I AM destroying the Jezebel spirit.**

One by one, **I AM destroying the Delilah spirit.**

One by one, **I AM destroying all spirits of witchcraft.**

One by one, **I AM destroying the Leviathan spirit.**

One by one, **I AM destroying the Antichrist spirit.**

One by one, **I AM destroying the generational curses and the ancestral curses.**

One by one, **I AM bringing by people to the end of themselves.**

One by one, **my Spirit is convicting my people of their detestable, ongoing sins.**

One by one, **by my Spirit, I AM bringing by people into total and utter repentance.**

One by one, **I AM setting my people free from yokes of slavery.**

One by one, **I AM rescuing my people from the religion that they have been trapped in.**

One by one, **I AM suddenly bringing my people into a personal, intimate, life-changing relationship with me.**

My Word says "Come close to me, and I will come close to you."

One by one, **I AM giving my people the revelation of the depth of my love for them.**

One by one, **I AM giving my people revelation that they are quite simply NOTHING WITHOUT ME.**

One by one, **I AM giving my people revelation that their purpose on earth is to BE ONE OF MY DISCIPLES.**

One by one, **I AM giving my people a revelation the SAME POWER that raised me from the dead lives in them.**

One by one, **I AM giving my people the revelation that it is not they that live, but I the Lord your God that lives in them.**

One by one, **I AM giving my people the revelation that greater is the spirit that is in them than the spirit that is in the world.**

One by one, **I AM giving my people the revelation that they have to seek my Kingdom and my righteousness first, and all else will be given to them.**

One by one, **I AM giving my people the revelation that every single day, to obey me, they have to freely give as they have freely received.**

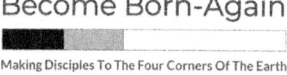

One by one, **I AM giving my people the revelation that every day, they need to deny themselves, pick up their cross and follow me.**

One by on, **I AM giving my people the revelation that when I say "Who will go for me? Who can I send?" they need to say "I will go Lord, send me."**

One by one, **I AM giving my people the revelation that their purpose on earth is to be my hands and feet and to DO MY WORK UPON THE EARTH every single day of their life.**

One by one, **I AM setting my people free from the prison of religion and bringing them in to an intimate, personal, life-changing relationship with me, the King of Glory.**

March 10th 2023

There Is No Imminent, Simultaneous "Rapture", Says The Lord

My beloved, from my mouth comes WISDOM. I the Lord your God are giving you the eyes to see and the ears to hear, what I am saying about what I am doing ONCE AGAIN across the earth.

WHAT IS HAPPENING NOW HAS HAPPENED BEFORE.

What will happen in the future has already happened, for I the Lord your God, the King of Glory, the first and the last, **I MAKE THE SAME THINGS HAPPEN OVER AND OVER AGAIN.**

Since early 2020, the people who have said that they are mine, who have been honouring me with their lips, HAVE HAD HEARTS THAT ARE FAR FROM ME. Because of this, I will once again astound these hypocrites with amazing wonders. The wisdom of the wise will pass away, and the intelligence of the intelligent will disappear.

Look around at the nation's! Look and be amazed, for I am doing something in your own day, something you wouldn't even believe, even if someone told you about it.

My beloved child, THERE IS NO IMMINENT, SIMULTANEOUS "Rapture".

I am ONCE AGAIN SHAKING THE HEAVENS AND THE EARTH.

Look! I am creating new heavens and a new earth, and no one will even think about the old ones anymore. Be glad, my beloved, rejoice forever in my creation. And look, I will create Jerusalem as a place of HAPPINESS. Her people will be a source of JOY. I will REJOICE over Jerusalem and DELIGHT in my people, including you, my beloved, and the sound of weeping and crying will be heard in it no more.

NO LONGER will babies die when only a few days old.

NO LONGER will adults die before they have lived a full life.

NO LONGER WILL PEOPLE BE CONSIDERED OLD AT 100!

Only the cursed will die that young.

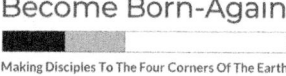

In these days you and all my people across the earth are living in today, people will live in the houses they build and eat the fruit of their own vineyards. Unlike the past, invaders will not take their houses and confiscate their vineyards. For my people will live as long as trees, and my chosen ones will have time to enjoy their hard won gains. They will not work in vain, and their children will not be doomed to misfortune. For they are people blessed by me, the Lord your God, the Sovereign Lord, and THEIR CHILDREN TOO WILL BE BLESSED.

I will answer them before they even call to me!

While they are still talking about their needs, I will go ahead and answer their prayers!

The wolf and the lamb will feed together. The lion will eat hay like a cow. But the snakes will eat dust. In those days, no one will be hurt or destroyed on my HOLY MOUNTAIN. I the Lord have spoken!

Hear this, you leaders of the people. Listen, all who live in the land. IN ALL YOUR HISTORY, HAS ANYTHING LIKE THIS EVER HAPPENED BEFORE?

Tell your children about it in the years to come, and tell your children to tell their children.

PASS THE STORY DOWN FROM GENERATION TO GENERATION.

My beloved child, you and all my people walking upon the stationary, flat earth that I created, your eyes have not seen, your ears have not heard and your minds have not yet conceived what I the Lord your God have got planned for you, for all those who love me.

My beloved child, I knew you before I formed you in your mother's womb. Before you were born, I set you apart and appointed you as my prophet to the nations. You may say, "Oh Sovereign Lord, I can't speak for you. I'm too young". But my beloved, FEARFULLY AND WONDERFULLY MADE SERVANT, don't say "I'm too young", for you must go wherever I send you and say whatever I tell you, and don't be afraid of the people. For I will be with you and will protect you. I the Lord have spoken!

As you are receiving my words now, I am reaching out and touching your mouth. LOOK, my beloved child, I have put my words in your mouth! Today I appoint you to

stand up against nations and kingdoms. Some you must uproot and tear down, destroy and overthrow. Others you must build up and plant.

Yes, my beloved child, before I created the heavens and the earth, I ordained for you to receive this message. Share this message with your brothers and sisters, for YES, I AM DOING A NEW THING!

A NEW AGE HAS BEGUN, and this new age began at the beginning of the year 2020, and remember, my beloved child, as you look around at the nations and be amazed, I am doing something in your own day, something you wouldn't even believe, even if someone told you about it.

Now GO! Tell others that the Kingdom of heaven is near. Heal the sick, cast out demons. Cure those with leprosy, and raise the dead. Give as freely as you have received, says I, the Sovereign Lord.

July 23rd 2023

You Are Waiting For Me, But I Am Waiting For You, Says The Lord

My beloved child, at the time of you receiving my message now, **you have been and you are waiting for me to move in your life.**

You are waiting for me to answer your prayers.

You are waiting for me to fulfil promises to you in my Word.

You are waiting for me to bring the breakthrough.

You are waiting for me to move in your life.

My beloved child, **I am waiting for you.**

I am waiting for you to move in your life.

I am waiting for you to face into your fear of man.

I am waiting for you to start living your life outside of your comfort zone.

I am waiting for you to step off the boat in faith.

I am waiting for you to walk by faith not by sight.

I am waiting for you to begin talking by faith, not by sight.

I am waiting for you to not just be a hearer of my Word, but to be a doer of my Word.

I am waiting for you to freely give as you have freely received.

I am waiting for you to start living your life worthy of the calling with which you have received.

Many are called but few are chosen, and **I have chosen you, my beloved child, to be one of my disciples.**

I have chosen you to be my hands and feet upon the earth where you live.

I have chosen you to be one of my glory carriers.

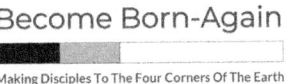

My beloved child, across the earth, throughout all countries, **there are hundreds of millions of my children** - men, women, teenagers and little children - but particularly men and women, who are waiting for me to move in their life, yet it is I the Lord your God that is waiting for them to move in their life.

My beloved child, what I am calling you to do is not difficult, is not challenging, is not burdensome.

My beloved child, I am calling you to begin going into the lives of people you have never met before, and as you look at them and smile because you love them and you know how much I love them, **I am asking you to say to them "Hi, God bless you! Do you know that Jesus loves you?"**

IT IS THAT SIMPLE.

I have put my Spirit into you, and **I have not given you a spirit of fear,** but of power, of love and of a sound mind.

It is not by your strength, it is not by your might, but it is by my Spirit that you will begin having conversations with complete strangers. **I will give you the words to say.** I will give you the responses to people's questions. **My Spirit will guide you** into sharing the most important and the most relevant parts of me giving you the revelation that you are one of my children, that you are chosen and not forsaken.

No longer in any way have a fear of man.

No longer in any way worry about what you might say to someone that you have never met before.

No longer worry about what they may say to you.

No longer worry about how they may react to you, for my beloved child, **NO WEAPONS FORMED AGAINST YOU WILL PROSPER, and every tongue that may rise up against you will condemn for that is a heritage of the servants of me the Lord of lords, the King of kings.**

My beloved child, **it is not you that live but I the Lord that live in you.**

No longer wait for me to move in your life.

No longer wait for the miracle breakthrough.

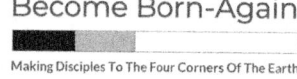

No longer wait for me to fulfil a promise from my Word.

No longer wait for me to answer your prayers.

GO OUT.

BE THE ANSWER TO OTHER PEOPLE'S PRAYERS.

Go out and shine light into other people's darkness.

Go out and freely give as you are freely received.

For everyone who calls on my name will be saved. **But how can the people that I am going to be sending you into the lives of, call out for me to save them, unless they believe in me?** And how will they believe in me unless they know about me? And how will they know about me unless someone tells them? And how will someone tell them unless they are sent?

My beloved child, I am sending YOU out in the place, in the area, in the country that you live because my Word tells you "How beautiful are the feet of messengers who bring Good News?"

My beloved child, I am waiting for you to take care of my business, and my promise to you my beloved child, is that whilst you are taking care of my business, I will take care of yours.

All my promises to you in my Word are "Yes and Amen" in my perfect time, **but remember, faith without works is dead.**

Works are being my hands and feet upon the Earth every single day.

When I ask, "Who will go for me? Who can I send?" **you will say my beloved child, "I will go! Send me!"**

You will speak when I ask you to speak.

You will go when I ask you to go.

You will offer to pray for someone when I ask you to offer to pray for that someone.

You will offer to lay hands on that person when I ask you to lay hands on that person.

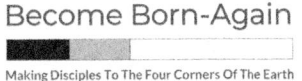

My beloved child, **live your life worthy of the calling with which you have received,** and that is to be one of my true disciples who I have chosen to be living in the time now, where I the Lord your God are once again shaking the heavens on the earth.

My Kingdom come, my will be done, on earth as it is in heaven, says I the Sovereign Lord.

May 30th 2023

Almost All Of My Chosen People Are Living Self-Centeredly, Says The Lord

My beloved child, you are receiving my message, for me to give you wisdom and revelation of how in 2023, the VAST MAJORITY of my Sons and Daughters who I have set free, who I have given the eyes to see and ears to hear, the VAST MAJORITY OF MY CHOSEN PEOPLE HAVE BEEN CONTINUING TO COMMIT MANY SINS.

These many sins are all connected, and these many sins have meant that my people have NOT been living their life worthy of the calling that they have received.

My Word tells you and all my people "Freely you have received, now freely give."

My Word tells you and all my people "It is not you that live but I the Lord your God that lives in you."

My Word tells you and all my people "I have not given you a spirit of fear, but of power, of love and of a sound mind."

My Word tells you and all my people "It is a sin to know what you ought to do and then not do it."

My Word tells you and all my people "To love your neighbour as yourself."

My Word tells you and all my people to "Love your enemies."

My Word tells you and all my people to "Go and proclaim that the Kingdom of Heaven has come near. Heal the sick. Cast out demons. Raise the dead. Cure those with leprosy. Freely give as you have freely received."

My Word tells you and all my people that "I am the one who comforts you, so why are you afraid of mere humans, who wither like the grass and disappear?"

My Word tells you and all my people "Do not fear people or their words. Don't be afraid even though their threats surround you like nettles and briars and stinging scorpions. Do not be dismayed by their dark scowls even though they are rebels."

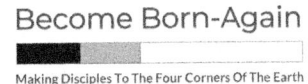

My Word tells you and all my people that "Fearing people is a dangerous trap. But trusting in me, the Lord your God, means safety."

My Word tells you and all my people that "I the Lord are for you, so that you should have no fear. What can mere people do to you?"

My beloved child, in 2023, almost all of my chosen people are living self-centredly.

THEY HAVE A FEAR OF MAN.

They are ashamed of the Gospel, which is the power of God that brings salvation to all who believe.

My Word tells you and all my people, that "Everyone who calls on my name will be saved. But how can they call on me to save them unless they believe in me? And how can they believe in me if they have never heard about me? And how can they hear about me unless someone tells them? And how will anyone go and tell them without being sent? That is why the Scriptures say "How beautiful are the feet of messengers who bring Good News."

My beloved child, NO LONGER HAVE A FEAR OF MAN.

NO LONGER live in your comfort zone.

NO LONGER be ashamed of the Gospel.

NO LONGER hold back from telling complete strangers about me the Lord your God.

Freely give as you have freely received.

Remember my beloved child, it is a sin to know what you ought to do and then not do it.

Do not be like your brothers and sisters who are ashamed of me, who are living with a fear of man. I have put my Spirit into you and greater is the Spirit that is in you than the spirit that is in the world.

I HAVE NOT GIVEN YOU A SPIRIT OF FEAR, but of power, of love and of a sound mind.

It is not you that live but I the Lord that lives in you, and I have called you by name from your mother's womb to be my hands and feet, to be one of my glory carriers, to be one of my disciples walking upon the earth, bringing my kingdom down upon the

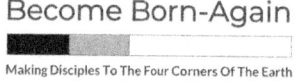

earth. Bringing my glory into more and more people's life, for I am the King of glory, and my will be done, on earth as it is in Heaven.

May 25th 2023

This Is Something Almost All Of My Chosen People Haven't Been Doing, Says The Lord

My beloved child, I am giving you wisdom and revelation of SOMETHING WHICH ALMOST ALL OF MY CHOSEN PEOPLE HAVEN'T BEEN DOING in their day-to-day life.

There are reasons that my chosen people haven't been doing this, and I am going to reveal what are the most common reasons so many of my people are struggling, are battling, are expecting, are waiting.

So many of my people are desperate for the breakthrough to come.

So many of my people are desperate for their circumstances to change.

So many of my people are desperate for their financial circumstances to improve.

So many of my people are desperate for their prodigal son or their prodigal daughter to come home.

So many of my people are desperate to see the miracle healing.

So many of my people are desperate to be delivered from the addiction that has been ruining their life.

So many of my people are desperate to see my promises to them fulfilled in their life.

So many of my people are desperate to feel my tangible presence more in their life.

So many of my people are desperate to hear my voice more in their day to day life.

So many of my people are desperate to experience my tangible presence and my glory manifest in their life.

So many of my people are desperate to experience what they see other people experiencing.

So many of my people are desperate to live in joy and peace.

So many of my people are desperate to see the chains of bondage and slavery broken in their life.

SO MANY OF MY PEOPLE ACROSS THE EARTH ARE DESPERATE.

So many of my people across the earth are waiting.

So many of my people across the earth are longing.

So many of my people across the earth are confused.

So many of my people across the earth are frustrated.

So many of my people across the earth are bewildered.

So many of my people across the earth are fearful.

So many of my people across the earth are doubting.

So many of my people across the earth are feeling consumed.

So many of my people across the earth are burdened.

So many of my people across the earth are not experiencing my glory in their life.

My beloved child, there is something that so many of my people across the Earth are not yet doing.

It is a sin for my people to know what they ought to do and then not do it.

This something that so many of my people across the Earth are not yet doing, IS TELLING COMPLETE STRANGERS ABOUT ME, THEIR LORD AND SAVIOUR.

So many of my people are living with THE FEAR OF MAN, and the fear of man is preventing them from telling people whom they have never met before about me, about my love and about what I did on the cross to save their life.

So many of my people are trying to take care of their own business, and in doing so they are not taking care of my business.

So many of my people are so consumed with their own life and their own circumstances and their own trials and tribulations, that they are NOT telling other people about me.

They are NOT sharing the Good News.

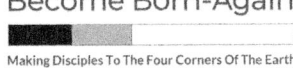

They are NOT sharing the Gospel.

They are NOT being my hands and feet.

They are NOT shining light into other people's darkness.

They are DENYING ME ON EARTH BEFORE MEN.

They are lukewarm, and my Word tells you and all my people that if you are lukewarm, neither cold nor hot, I WILL VOMIT YOU OUT OF MY MOUTH.

My beloved child, when you and your brothers and your sisters, when you step out of your comfort zone, when you face into your fears of telling complete strangers about me, YOU BEGIN TO EXPERIENCE MY GLORY.

You begin to bring my glory down from heaven into other people's lives.

You begin to realise and comprehend the significance of your life here upon the earth as my hands and feet.

You begin to realise that your life is not about yourself, it is not about your own circumstances. YOUR LIFE IS ABOUT SERVING ME.

YOUR LIFE is about being one of my glory carriers.

YOUR LIFE is about sharing the Good News.

YOUR LIFE is about shining light into other people's darkness.

YOUR LIFE is about being one of my disciples, for I have called you by name from your mother's womb to be one of my disciples, to be one of my glory carriers, to be my hands and feet.

CAN YOU NOW SEE?

Can you know see THE REASON WHY SO MANY OF MY PEOPLE ACROSS THE EARTH HAVE NOT BEEN EXPERIENCING MY GLORY?

They have not been seeing the breakthrough.

They have not been feeling my presence, my love, my joy.

So many of my people have been living in bondage, in chains, in slavery, in a place of TIMIDITY, in a place of FEAR.

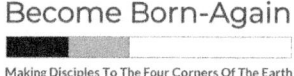

SO MANY OF MY PEOPLE HAVE NOT YET STARTED LIVING THEIR LIFE WORTHY OF THE CALLING THAT THEY HAVE RECEIVED - the same calling that you have received, TO BE ONE OF MY GLORY CARRIERS.

My beloved child, NOW GO. When I asked you, "Who can I send? Who will go for me?" may you say to me, "I will go Lord, SEND ME. I will speak to whoever you want me to speak to. I will offer to pray for whoever you want me to pray for. I will be your hands and feet upon the Earth every single day."

Thank you, my beloved child for hearing and receiving my words to you now.

Remember, it is not you that live but I the Lord that lives in you.

You can do and you will do all things through me, the Lord your God who gives you strength.

I have not given you a spirit of fear, but of power, of love and of a sound mind, and as you experience divine encounter after divine encounter, you will begin to experience me pouring out my love into you. My RIVERS OF LIVING WATERS are being poured out into you so that my rivers of living waters will be flowing from your heart into the lives of people whom you have never met before.

My beloved child, I HAVE ONLY JUST BEGUN pouring my Spirit out upon all flesh.

I HAVE ONLY JUST BEGUN bringing in my new age.

I HAVE ONLY JUST BEGUN shaking once again the heavens and the earth, and your eyes haven't seen, your ears haven't heard and your mind has not yet conceived what I the Lord your God have got planned for you because you love me.

My Kingdom come, my will be done, on earth as it is in heaven, says I the Sovereign Lord.

July 23rd 2023

There Is Going To Be Repentance On A Scale Unseen Before, Says The Lord

My beloved child, you are receiving my message here, for I the Lord your God desire to give you wisdom and revelation of **the reason why almost all of the Christians across the flat, stationery earth that I created, LISTEN TO MAN AND NOT ME.**

From early in the year 2020, **I have shone my light into the darkness of the established church systems.**

I have given everyone across the earth a shocking exposure of the scale and depth of sin of my bride.

It is a SIN to know what you ought to do and then not do it.

In 2020 I revealed that there was an **incredibly small percentage of my followers who were born again, baptised, filled with my Spirit, who had their faith in me the Lord your God and in me alone.**

What there **HAS** to be, and what there **WILL** be by my Spirit, through conviction by my Spirit, **there is going to be REPENTANCE within my body on a scale unlike anyone walking the earth today has ever experienced before.**

It is not just going to be confession of sins, **it is going to be repentance.**

As I convict more and more and more men, women, teenagers and children of **their detestable sins,** there will be **absolute repentance with the entirety of their beings.**

When I reveal to people living in sin, **all the decisions that they have made in their life** whilst they have been my follower, but they have had their faith in man, and not me, the King of kings, the Lord of lords - **be prepared my beloved child, be prepared for you to see with your own eyes and for you to hear and for you to watch through social media, more and more and more people FALLING TO THEIR KNEES, as the WEIGHT of my glory, as the WEIGHT of my presence, as the WEIGHT of my unfailing love, as the WEIGHT of my holiness falls upon them, and**

they will be in floods of tears in total and absolute repentance of the detestable sins that they have continued to commit.

There is going to be more and more and more people **renouncing the things that they and their family members have been a part of**.

The chains of slavery are being destroyed.

The yokes of bondage are being destroyed.

Generational curses are being destroyed.

Ancestral curses are being destroyed.

The spirit of witchcraft is being destroyed.

The Jezebel spirit is being destroyed.

The Leviathan spirit is being destroyed.

The Delilah spirit is being destroyed.

The ANTICHRIST SPIRIT is being destroyed in the lives of more and more and more men, women and children, for MY KINGDOM COME, MY WILL BE DONE, on earth as it is in heaven.

My beloved child, **through that conviction of sin, both sins that are public and sins that are hidden in darkness,** this will lead to **confession** of sin, this will lead to **renouncing** everything that my people have been a part of, and this will lead on to **absolute repentance from the entirety of their being** - and **THEN AND ONLY THEN when my people have truly died to themselves,** when my people are now ready to deny themselves, to pick up their cross daily and follow me, **it will be only then that MY POWER AND MY GLORY is going to be seen in their life.**

And you my beloved child, I have chosen **YOU** to be one of my glory carriers.

I am the King of glory, and I have put my Spirit into you, and I am putting my Spirit into more and more and more men, women and children, **AND MY GLORY IS COMING UPON THE EARTH IN GREATER AND GREATER WAYS.**

I AM GOING TO BE MOVING IN POWER UNSEEN BEFORE.

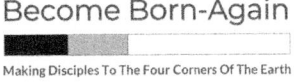

Your eyes have not seen, your ears have not heard and your mind has not yet conceived what I the King of Glory have got planned and prepared for you and **ALL MY CHOSEN PEOPLE ACROSS THE EARTH**, because you love me.

Look around at the nations! Look and be amazed, for I am doing something in your own day, something that you wouldn't even believe even if someone told you about it.

Hear this you leaders of the people. Listen all who live in the land. **IN ALL YOUR HISTORY, HAVE YOU EVER SEEN ANYTHING LIKE THIS BEFORE?**

Tell your children about it in the years to come, and tell your children to tell their children.

Pass the story down of I the King of Glory bringing in a new age from the beginning of 2020, from generation to generation, says I the Sovereign Lord, the Holy One of Israel.

March 16th 2022

I Had To Send The Locusts Into Your Life To Destroy Your Old Wineskins, Says The Lord

My beloved Sons and Daughters, this is the Lord your God. I have called you by name. You are chosen and not forsaken. It has been I the Lord your God that have carried you through every moment of your life. It has been I that have allowed you to experience every single thing that you have experienced, because I have got a calling that is upon your life.

I waste nothing. You have experienced things in your life that many other people would not have been able to survive. It has been I the Lord your God that have brought you through everything, I have carried you in my arms. I work in ALL THINGS FOR GOOD for those who love me and those who live according to my purpose for them, and as I am pouring into my spirit, as I am revealing to you that I have plans for your life, and they are plans for good and not for disaster to give you a future and a hope, I am revealing to you now that the pains, the trauma, the trials and the tribulations of your past are going to be used to help more and more people for their future.

I am your healer. Right now I am doing a deep work within you. I am healing you, the entirety of your being, your heart is now a heart of flesh and it is no longer a heart of stone. I am now breaking the iron bars. I am breaking the chains of bondage. I am breaking the chains to your past, for I the Lord of Heaven's Armies has spoken.

Through your surrender to me, through repenting of your sins, it is I the Lord your God that have set you apart. Your identity is in me and in me alone. You are fearfully and wonderfully made in my image. I am the mighty warrior that saves. I have gone before you. I will never leave you nor forsake you. I am the one that opens doors that no man can shut. I am the one who shuts doors that no man can open. It has been I the Lord your God that has been in the furnace with you. As you have been

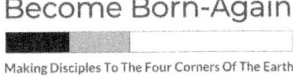

going through the greatest trials and tribulations and pressings and crushings of your entire life, like Shadrach, Meshach and Abednego, you have not been burnt up because I the Lord your God have only allowed you to go through what I knew you would get through.

The testing of your faith produces perseverance, and you have had your faith tested, but now as I am revealing more to you of what I am doing in your life, the painful process and experience that you have been through in your life, where it has been I that has sent the locusts into your life because the locusts have been destroying your old wineskins. Everything connected to your past, your life experiences, the pains, the feelings, the emotions, the negative thoughts, the traumas of your past, all of those are part of your old wineskins and the locusts have been destroying your old wineskins, because I do not pour out my new wine into old wineskins. I do not bring you my glory, my provisions, my miracles, signs and wonders into your old self because your old self would not have been able to cope with everything that I have planned to do in your life. Instead the locusts have had to destroy your old wineskins.

I have had to bring you to this place of submission, of surrender, the place where now as I have been creating in you your new wineskins, I am now preparing to pour into you my new wine.

Provision unlike you have seen before.

Breakthrough online you have seen before.

Healing online you have seen before.

Miracles, signs and wonders online you have seen before.

My hand is mighty upon your life. I have anointed your head with oil. I am pouring into you now my spirit. More wisdom than you have ever experienced before, and from this moment, as you read my words, I will be giving you deep revelations. My word is going to be coming alive unlike you have ever experienced before. As you are filled with my spirit, as you hear and listen to worship music, you will be worshipping me in spirit and in truth and I will be leading you into floods of tears, because these are tears of breakthrough, these are tears of healing, these are tears

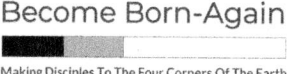

of deliverance, these are tears of joy, these are tears knowing that I have plans for your life and those plans are plans for good and not for disaster to give you a future and a hope.

Your faith comes by hearing and hearing by my word. Your faith is going to be in me and in me alone. I am the bread of life and so I'm calling you to come to me, to come to the well, to receive my living waters so my living waters will flow from your belly, that you will be my glory carrier, filled with my spirit. It is not you that live, but I that live in you.

I have set you apart. You are chosen. I have set you apart in your entire family, and you have been through pain, trauma, trials, tribulations. But I the Lord of Heaven's Armies I come to cause division, because I have to separate out the wheat from the shaft, the sheep from the goats. I have to do it. I have to separate out those that are living in fear, and those are living in faith. I have to separate those who are still bound by the god of the world and those who are set apart by me, filled with my spirit, saved by my grace, and you have been set apart, filled with my spirit, saved by my grace.

My grace and my mercy has always been upon your life and now you are experiencing more than ever before my unfailing Agape love. I am pouring into you now my love, my peace which surpasses all understanding which guards your heart and your mind in Christ Jesus, me, the Lord your God.

My spirit upon you is going to be leading and guiding you more precisely than ever before. You will see that my spirit is guiding you and leading you into my Word, into precisely the words that you need to read so that I can reveal more and more to you of the calling upon your life and what I am doing in your life and what I am doing across the earth. You are now going to begin seeing truly that my hand is in everything, that I work in all things.

You will never again feel helpless or hopeless or fearful. I have not given you a spirit of fear, but of power, of love and of a sound mind, and my perfect love for you expels all fear.

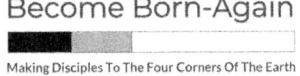

I have chosen you to be my faithful servant, to be my hands and feet. To walk by faith and not by sight, and as I open doors that no man can shut, as you begin to walk through those doors, I will be bringing you into a place of awe and wonder. Your breakthroughs are coming. Miracle breakthroughs are coming in your life. Miracle healings are going to be manifesting in your life and the lives of your family members. You are going to be praying and interceding unlike ever before.

I have given you all authority to trample upon lions and cobras, to crush fierce lions and serpents under your feet. You have all the authority in the spirit realm, through your faith in me and through my blood that I shed on the cross for you for your sins and for the sins of the world. Death is defeated. You are no longer a slave to your sin nature, you are a child of God. You are mine, says I, the Lord of Heaven's Armies, and your eyes haven't seen your ears, haven't heard and your mind hasn't conceived what I the Lord your God have got planned for you because you love me.

Trust in me and you will see that I will bring to pass the desires of your heart, because I the Lord your God have placed those desires in your heart. Trust in me, trust in my Word, trust in my plans for your life, trust in my way because my way is perfect. And be patient, as you wait for me to move and as you trust in my perfect timing, says I the Lord of Heaven's Armies.

June 21st 2023

So, So Many Of My Followers Have Faith That Is Dead For They Have No Works, Says The Lord

My beloved child, my Word tells you that **it is impossible to please me without faith**. You know that faith is a substance of things hoped for, **the evidence of things not seen**.

My Word also tells you and all my people across the earth, that **FAITH WITHOUT WORKS IS DEAD**.

Works are **not just** good deeds.

Works are **not just** wearing a cross on your neck.

Works are **not just** sharing my Word on social media.

Works are **not just** gathering with your brothers and sisters.

Works are **not just** praying to me in the secret place.

Works are **not just** worshipping in spirit and in truth.

Works are **not just** interceding for non-believers.

WORKS ARE BEING MY HANDS AND FEET.

Works are talking to complete strangers about my love for them.

Works are offering to pray for people you have only just met.

Works are talking by faith, not by sight.

Works are trusting in me and my Word completely.

Works are living with joy and peace every day.

Works are considering it an opportunity for great joy when trials of any kind come your way.

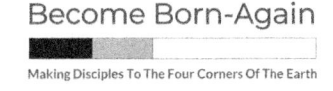

Works are not to being ashamed of the Gospel.

Works are you be willing to go when I ask you to go.

Works are you being willing to speak when I ask you to speak.

Works are you living outside of your comfort zone

Works are you no longer having a fear of man

Works are operating in the gifts of my Spirit.

Works are offering to lay hands on people for me to heal them.

Works are going into someone's life to share a word of knowledge.

Works are speaking prophetically into someone's life.

My beloved child, **it is a sin to know what you ought to do and then not do it.**

My Word is so clear - **if you are lukewarm**, neither cold nor hot, **I will vomit you out of my mouth.**

So, so, so many of **my followers have faith that is currently dead, for they have no works.**

Instead, they are living with a fear of man.

I haven't given any of my people a spirit of fear, but of power, of love and of a sound mind.

My beloved child, may each day you **desire to have faith AND works.**

My beloved child, **be my hands and feet.**

My beloved child, **trust in me, trust in my Word, trust in my promises to you.**

ALL my promises to you are yes and amen, **in my perfect time**.

Show your brothers and sisters, **your faith AND your works**, says I the Sovereign Lord.

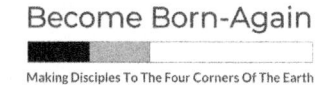

January 7th 2023

This Is MY SEPARATION Of People, Says The Lord

My beloved, my Word tells you that I come not to bring peace, but to bring a SWORD.

Can you see it?

Can you feel it?

Are you experiencing the SEPARATION that I started in early 2020?

This is MY SEPARATION OF PEOPLE.

How they live.

How they act.

How they behave.

WHO THEY SERVE.

The SEPARATION between people living ungodly lives, and my people living godly lives.

The SEPARATION between people living with a fear of man, and my people living only with a reverent fear of me the Lord your God.

The SEPARATION between people living in sin, and my people living righteously.

The SEPARATION between spiritually dead churches, and on-fire Holy Spirit filled gatherings of my true born-again followers.

The SEPARATION between people living self-righteously, and my people knowing that their righteousness comes from me, and me alone.

The SEPARATION of people living in the world and loving things in the world, and my people who do not love the world nor the things in it.

The SEPARATION between the lukewarm followers of me, and my on-fire, spirit-filled, totally surrendered glory carriers.

The SEPARATION between people living with pride, and my people living in total and complete humility.

The SEPARATION between people saying they have prophetic messages of what's to come and those messages are of doomsday, apocalyptical sorrow, tribulation and hell on earth, messages not from me, and my chosen prophets who are truly surrendered to me, who are living with total humility, and who are receiving every day messages from me, from my heart, to give to my people.

The SEPARATION between people talking about and sharing messages of fear and Doomsday apocalyptical messages, and my chosen people talking about and sharing messages of how MY GLORY IS MANIFESTING UPON THE EARTH MORE AND MORE AND MORE.

The SEPARATION between people focusing on the things of the world, and my chosen people fixing their eyes on me and focusing on the things above, not the things below.

The SEPARATION between people giving the enemy authority, and my chosen people giving me the King of kings, the Lord of lords, ALL the glory, ALL the praise and ALL the honour, for I am Sovereign.

The SEPARATION of my followers who have been deceived and indoctrinated by man, and my chosen people who have been willing to let go of every single thing that sinful, deceitful man has ever taught them.

The SEPARATION between people unwilling to step out of their comfort zone, and my chosen people willing to live outside of their comfort zone.

The SEPARATION between people who have one foot in the world and one foot in faith, and my chosen people whose faith is in me, the Lord your God, and IN ME ALONE.

The SEPARATION between my followers who still have a veil of deception over them, and my chosen people who I have completely set free from every deception and every lie and all the indoctrination that my people have experienced throughout their entire lives.

The SEPARATION between people who don't see and who don't want to see the power of my Spirit at work, and my chosen people who are BEGINNING to experience the POWER OF MY SPIRIT MANIFEST in their life and the lives of people across the earth.

The SEPARATION between people still believing the globe deception, and my chosen people who I have set free from the globe deception, and they know that the earth that I created is fixed, immovable and will not be moved.

The SEPARATION between my followers who are bound by religious spirits, and my chosen people who are totally and completely free from all religious spirits.

The SEPARATION of people who I haven't yet given the eyes to see and ears to hear, and my chosen people who are totally and completely free in me, the Lord your God.

My beloved child, CONTINUE TO FIX YOUR EYES ON ME.

Continue to read my Word every day.

Continue to worship me in spirit and in truth every day.

Continue to listen to me and not man.

Continue to walk by faith not by sight.

Continue to talk by faith not by sight.

Know that BY MY SWORD, as I have created this division amongst people, one by one all those people who are not yet completely surrendered to me, I am sending into the valley of judgement.

One by one, I am coming down from Heaven, mounted on a mighty angelic being, to rescue my people, my lost sheep, from the deep waters, and I am SUDDENLY setting them free.

I am SUDDENLY filling them with my Spirit.

They are SUDDENLY being baptised by my Spirit.

My beloved child, my chosen servant, never have doubt about this. You are living in and through, and I have called you from your mother's womb to be a part of, MY WORLDWIDE REFORMATION.

I, the Lord your God, the King of Glory, HAVE ONLY JUST BEGUN.

Your eyes have not seen, your ears have not heard and your mind has not yet conceived what I the Lord your God have got planned for you because you love me.

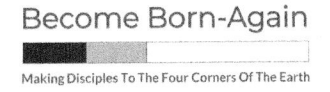

Thank you, my beloved, for receiving my message to you now.

My will be done, on earth, as it is in heaven, says I, the Sovereign Lord.

February 14th 2023

The Gross Darkness That Has Covered The Earth For Hundreds Of Years Is Being Exposed, Says The Lord

My beloved child, I have planned and ordained for you to receive my message here, for I am giving you wisdom and understanding of what is taking place across the earth.

Many, many, many people, both my followers and those who I have awakened to some truth since early 2020, many people have said the world is getting darker.

My beloved child, FOR HUNDREDS OF YEARS A GROSS DARKNESS HAD COVERED THE EARTH, and before the year 2020, the darkness had been getting darker and darker, but most of the world darkness was hidden. It was not in plain sight.

The DEPRAVITY OF MAN, the SINFULNESS OF MAN, was HIDDEN behind people's smiles, behind people's lifestyle, behind people's jobs, behind people's careers, behind people's families, behind closed doors.

The CORRUPTION WITHIN THE WORLD SYSTEMS was hidden from most people across the earth.

The MOST DESPICABLE, EVIL THINGS THAT MAN DOES was mainly hidden from the view of most people across the earth.

Yes, my beloved child, there has been such a gross darkness covering the earth, as I HAVE ALLOWED THE SIN OF MAN TO POLLUTE ALL AREAS OF SOCIETY.

But then, from the start of the year 2020, I the Lord your God, the King of kings, the Lord of lords, the Alpha and the Omega, the first and the last, the beginning and the end, I BEGAN TO SHINE LIGHT IN TO THAT GROSS DARKNESS.

THE LIGHT ALWAYS SHINES IN THE DARKNESS, and the darkness can NEVER put it out.

Have no doubt about it, my beloved child, and tell your brothers and sisters too - THE WORLD IS NOT GETTING DARKER.

The GROSS DARKNESS that had covered the earth for hundreds of years IS BEING EXPOSED.

The SIN OF MAN has been getting EXPOSED for three years.

I have been REVEALING the hearts of man.

I have been revealing which people have been bowing down to man - which people are living with A FEAR OF MAN, and not a reverent fear of me, the one who holds them in the palm of my hand, the one who sustains their very existence.

One by one I am coming down from heaven, down into the deep waters, into the miry clay, to rescue my people from all their enemies.

One by one I am lifting the veil.

One by one I am setting the captives free.

One by one the scales are falling from people's eyes.

EVERYTHING DONE IN DARK IS BEING BROUGHT INTO THE LIGHT, says I the Lord of lords, the King of glory.

MY GLORY IS COMING UPON THE EARTH IN WAYS IN WHICH MY PEOPLE HAVE NEVER EXPERIENCED BEFORE.

HAVE NO FEAR. I have not given you a spirit of fear, but of power, of love and of a sound mind.

EACH DAY SPEAK LIKE.

DO NOT ALLOW words of DARKNESS, words of DEATH, words of DEVASTATION, words of DESTRUCTION, words of FEAR to come from your lips.

SPEAK LIFE, MY BELOVED CHILD.

SPEAK MY WORD. DECLARE MY WORD. DECREE MY WORD. STAND ON MY WORD.

As I pour my Spirit into you now, BLAZING COALS OF FIRE ARE GOING TO BE COMING FROM YOUR TONGUE, and your words, your words which are going to be my words, are going to be PENETRATING THE DARKNESS, are going to be DESTROYING DEMONIC ALTERS, DEMONIC STRONGHOLDS.

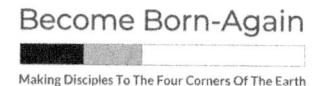

STRONGMEN ARE GETTING BOUND UP AND DESTROYED.

EVERY SINGLE DEMON IS BEING EXPOSED AND CAST OUT IN MY NAME, says I the King of kings, the Lord of lords.

My beloved child, I have put my spirit into you, and GREATER IS THE SPIRIT THAT IS IN YOU THAN THE SPIRIT THAT IS IN THE WORLD.

I HAVE MADE YOU THE HEAD AND NOT THE TAIL.

I HAVE NOT GIVEN YOU A SPIRIT OF FEAR, BUT OF POWER, OF LOVE AND OF A SOUND MIND.

I have given you ALL AUTHORITY to trample upon lions and cobras, to crush fierce lions and serpents under your feet.

You resist the devil and he flees from you.

I am sanctifying you.

I am making you MORE AND MORE AND MORE IN TO MY IMAGE.

YOU ARE by hands and feet.

YOU ARE my glory carrier.

YOU ARE my disciple, says I the Sovereign Lord.

For my Word tells you in Matthew 21:22, YOU CAN PRAY FOR ANYTHING, and if you have faith YOU WILL RECEIVE IT, and as you receive my words to you now, I am releasing into your life FAITH IN ME THAT IS ABSOLUTELY PURE.

YOU WILL NEVER AGAIN HAVE FAITH IN MAN.

YOUR FAITH IS GOING TO BE IN ME the Lord your God and IN ME ALONE.

YOU WILL NOT BOW DOWN TO MAN.

You are not living upon the earth to please man. You are living to please me, for is you are living to please man, you would not be my servant.

YOU are my masterpiece.

I created YOU in my image.

YOU are fearfully and wonderfully made.

It is not you that live, but I THAT LIVE IN YOU.

NOW GO, my beloved child. Share the Good News, cast out demons, heal the sick and proclaim that the Kingdom of Heaven is near, says I the Sovereign Lord.

October 3rd 2022

My Beloved Child, I Know Why You Have Been Unable To Forgive, Says The Lord

My beloved, I know that you have been unable to forgive. For what you have experienced in your life, I know why you have been unable to forgive.

Up until you receiving my message to you, the unforgiveness that you have carried with you, the unforgiveness that has been impossible for you to break free from, it is going to be by you coming to me and saying "Lord, help me to forgive", that through my Spirit, you will finally be able to forgive. You will finally be completely free from your past life experiences.

My promise to you, my beloved child, is through your total surrender of everything that you've battled with in your life, through your total surrender to me, and by you, with all your heart, desiring to make me the Lord over your life, my promise to you is that I am going to give you a new heart. I the Lord I am going to take out your stony heart, stony because of what you have experienced, because of how others have treated you, and I am going to be giving you a new heart, and your new heart is a heart of flesh.

I the Lord, I am the only one that can break you out of that prison of unforgiveness.

I the Lord are the only one that can bring you peace which surpasses all understanding.

My beloved child, my heart's desire for you is for you to live in joy and peace.

Your life up until this moment has led you to believe that your identity is based upon your whole life experiences, that your identity is connected to the pains, to the trials, to the dark valleys, to the suffering that you have experienced in your life.

My beloved, as you are receiving my words to you now, I am giving you the eyes to see, the ears to hear and a new heart to allow you to receive all my unfailing love.

Your identity, my beloved child, is in me, the Lord your God, and in me alone. I am the only one that can bring you total healing from your past life experiences. It is only by my Spirit that you are going to be able to forgive, and following your forgiveness, by the power of my Spirit, you will be able to pray for the salvation of those who have hurt you in your life.

It is I the Lord your God that has carried you through every single moment of your life.

It is I the Lord your God that carried you through those dark valleys.

It is I the Lord your God that gave you the strength to keep going.

It is I the Lord your God that brought you back when you were on the verge of taking your own life.

It is I the Lord your God that have called you by name. I have called you by name not just to believe in me, but to become my glory carrier, to be my hands and feet, and you will see my beloved child, in my perfect time, not only will you have completely forgiven those whom you haven't been able to forgive before now, you will also pray with all your heart for their salvation, but above all of this, you will be living your life worthy of the calling that you have received, and that calling my beloved child, is to be my glory carrier, to be my hands and feet.

I am waiting my beloved, for you to bring your unforgiveness to the cross, says I the Sovereign Lord.

January 16th 2023

I Know The Reasons Why You Have Been Unable To Love & Forgive Yourself, Says The Lord

My beloved child, I know the reasons why you have been unable to forgive yourself. I know the reasons why you have been unable to love yourself.

My beloved child, I am calling you now to TOTALLY AND COMPLETELY FOCUS ON ME.

The greatest commandment that I have given is to love me, the Lord your God, with all your heart, with all your mind, with all your soul and with all your strength, and to love your neighbour as yourself.

My beloved child, see how I am not commanding you to love yourself?

Your righteousness comes through me, the Lord your God, and through me alone.

I shed my blood on the cross, so that you can be forgiven for all your sins, so that you can be washed white as snow, so that you can receive salvation by grace, through your faith in me the Lord your God, and through receiving me as your Lord and Saviour.

Before I created the heavens and the earth, I planned and ordained for you to be receiving my message to you now.

Due to the sins of your past, you have been living in a prison. You have been surrounded by iron bars, by prison gates, and my beloved child, you have been living with a heart of stone, and your heart of stone has been COMPLETELY WRAPPED IN CHAINS TO YOUR PAST.

What I the Lord are doing right now as you are receiving my words, for I have given you the eyes to see and the ears to hear, I have lifted the veil for you, the scales have fallen from your eyes, and what I am doing now, I the Lord, by my devouring fire, I am DESTROYING THOSE PRISON BARS. I am DESTROYING THOSE IRON GATES right now, through my Word.

Right now as you are receiving my words, by my Spirit, I am DESTROYING EVERY SINGLE CHAIN THAT HAS BEEEN WRAPPED AROUND YOUR HEART OF STONE.

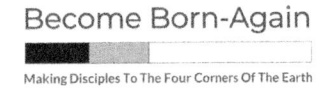

Remember my beloved, your heart of stone is a part of your old self, is a part of your old wineskins.

Now with your heart of stone exposed, I am taking out of you your heart of stone now, and I am giving you a new tender, responsive heart of flesh.

My beloved child, let the tears flow.

The tears are tears of breakthrough. Your tears are tears of receiving from me by my Spirit, your new heart. A HEART OF FLESH THAT HASN'T EXPERIENCED PAIN AND TRAUMA. Your heart of flesh that hasn't been affected by the sins of your past.

My beloved child, YOUR IDENTITY ISN'T IN YOUR PAST.

Your identity isn't in how people have treated you.

Your identity isn't in how you have treated other people.

Your identity isn't in the decisions that you have made in your past.

Your identity isn't in your family.

Your identity isn't in your appearance.

YOUR IDENTITY ISN'T IN THE SINS OF YOUR PAST.

My beloved, fearfully and wonderfully made child, YOUR IDENTITY IS IN ME THE LORD YOUR GOD, AND IN ME ALONE.

I have put my Spirit into you, and greater is the spirit that is in you than the spirit that is in the world.

My beloved child, FIX YOUR EYES ON ME.

Love me with ALL your heart, ALL your mind, ALL your soul and ALL your strength, and desire to truly love your neighbour as yourself.

Focus on the things of heaven, not the things of earth.

Focus on the things above, not the things below.

Focus on me and focus on my Word, for the more that you are focusing on me and my Word, the more that my Spirit is being stirred up inside of you, and the less you will be in your flesh, battling with feelings and emotions.

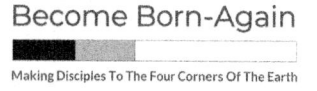

Come, worship me in spirit and in truth.

Raise your arms to the air.

Get down onto your knees.

SURRENDER EVERYTHING IN YOUR LIFE TO ME.

Cast ALL your burdens upon me, my beloved child, for I care for you, for my yoke is easy and my burden is light.

You are my masterpiece, and I know the plans that I have for you, they are plans for good and not for disaster, to give you a future and a hope.

November 30th 2022

You Are No Longer In Any Way Going To Be Living With Unforgiveness, Says The Lord

My beloved child, you know that my Word tells you that three things remain - faith, hope, and love, these three, and the greatest of these is love.

You know that the two most important commandments are to love me with all your heart, with all your mind, with all your soul, with all your strength, and to love your neighbour as yourself.

The reason that you are receiving my message to you now, is that I have called you by name from your mother's womb to truly embody and live the rest of your life following those two greatest commandments.

As you are receiving my words now, I am pouring my Spirit into you, and my devouring fire is destroying the remaining chains that have been around your heart. I am the chain breaker. Every chain of bondage breaks in my name.

My beloved child, you are no longer in any way going to be living with unforgiveness, for now what I am doing, is taking out of you your heart of stone, and giving you a new tender, responsive heart. A new heart of flesh, for what you say flows from what's in your heart.

And now, as you have received by faith your new heart of flesh, you will begin to truly embody my love for my chosen people, my love for all people.

No longer will anyone in your life or that will come into your life be able to offend you, will be able to hurt you, will be able to steal your joy, for no weapons formed against you will prosper and every tongue that rises up against you, you will condemn for that is a heritage of the servants of me the Lord your God.

My beloved, fearfully and wonderfully made child, I have called you by name from your mother's womb to be my glory carrier, to be my hands and feet.

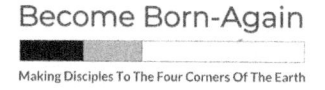

From this moment moving forward, following you receiving by faith your new heart of flesh, my Word is going to come alive in your heart unlike you have ever experienced before. Through you reading my Word yourself personally, I will be giving you wisdom and revelation in ways you have never experienced before.

As you listen to anointed worship music, the words are going to be speaking to you on a more deeper, on a more profound, on a more personal level than you have ever experienced before.

My beloved, expect me to bring you into tears of joy, tears because I am speaking to you and you are hearing on the inside of you by my Spirit, me speak to you throughout every single day.

The depth of intimacy of your relationship with me the Lord your God is now going to levels in which you have never experienced before.

Thank you, my beloved precious child for receiving my words by faith.

Thank you for everything you have already done for my kingdom, and thank you my beloved child for living your life worthy of the calling that you have received.

My will be done, on earth as it is in heaven, in your life and in the lives of every man, woman and child walking the earth, says I, the Sovereign Lord.

April 27th 2023

You Must Forgive Them So That You Will Be Forgiven, Says The Lord

My beloved child, I desire to give you wisdom and revelation about the men and women who have been complicit in bringing fear upon other people.

Since early 2020, I have allowed everything that has been taking place, for it has revealed the DEPRAVITY OF MAN. It has revealed that as my Word says, "The love of money truly is the root of all evil."

My beloved child, I have given you the eyes to see and the ears to hear. I have given you revelation already, that you have been lied to through your entire life by sinful, deceitful man, and your parents too and grandparents have been lied to through their entire lives too by sinful, deceitful man.

But my beloved, my Word tells you that the proud trust in themselves and their lives are crooked. WEALTH IS TREACHEROUS and the arrogant are never at rest. They open their mouths as wide as the grave, and like death, they are never satisfied. In their greed they have gathered up many nations and swallowed many peoples. But soon, their captors will taunt them. They will mock them saying "What sorrow awaits you thieves. Now you will get what you deserve. You became rich by extortion. But how much longer can this go on?"

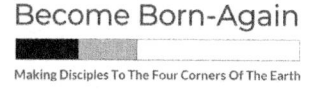

SUDDENLY their debtors will take action. They will turn on them and take all they have, while they stand trembling and helpless. Because they have plundered many nations, now all the survivors will plunder them. They committed murder throughout the countryside and filled the towns with violence. What sorrow awaits those who build big houses with money gained dishonestly. They believe their wealth will buy security, putting their family's nest beyond the reach of danger. But by the murders they have committed, they have shamed their name and forfeited their lives. The very stones in the walls cry out against them, and the beams in their ceilings echo the complaints. What sorrow awaits those who build cities with money gained through murder and corruption. Have I the Lord of Heaven's Armies promised that the wealth of nations will turn to ashes? They work so hard, but all in vain. For as the waters fill the sea, the earth will be filled with an awareness of my glory, for I am the King of Glory.

My beloved child, you know what I said on the cross. "Forgive them Father for they know not what they do."

My beloved, you must forgive them, so that you can be forgiven.

No longer do I desire for you to have any RESENTMENT, any BITTERNESS, any JEALOUSY, any UNFORGIVENESS towards people who have been complicit in bringing fear upon other people.

Instead, my beloved child, as my Word tells you, I urge you to pray for all people, to ask me to help them, to give me thanks, to intercede on their behalf, and to pray this way for kings and all who are in authority - all who are in positions of power and influence - so that you can live a quiet and peaceful lives marked by dignity and godliness, for this is good and pleases your Father in heaven, WHO WANTS EVERYONE TO BE SAVED AND TO UNDERSTAND THE TRUTH.

Remember, there is only one God and one mediator who can reconcile God and humanity. Myself, the Lord Jesus.

I GAVE MY LIFE TO PURCHASE FREEDOM FOR EVERYONE.

April 30ʰ 2023

My Shepherd, NEVER AGAIN Will You Preach A Watered-Down Gospel, Says The Lord

My beloved shepherd, I AM the Good Shepherd.

It is I the Lord your God that chose YOU to be one of my SHEPHERDS OF MY SHEEP.

I have chosen YOU to receive my message now, as I am ONCE AGAIN shaking the heavens and the earth.

In 2020, the previous age came to an end, and I, the Lord of lords, the King of kings, the one given the name above all names, I BEGAN TO SHINE LIGHT INTO THE GROSS DARKNESS that had covered the earth for hundreds of years.

I began to shine my light into THE GROSS DARKNESS THAT HAD COVERED MY CHURCH.

I began to shine my light into THE GROSS DARKNESS THAT HAD BEEN THE SIN OF MAN.

Since before I created the heavens and the earth, it has been MY DIVINE WILL to begin in 2020, EXPOSING THE STATE OF MY CHURCH.

People across the entire flat, stationary Earth that I created, have seen that ALMOST EVERY CHURCH, ALMOST EVERY PASTOR, ALMOST EVERY CHURCH LEADER, ALMOST EVERY ELDER, ALMOST EVERYONE IN A POSITION OF INFLUENCE WITHIN MY CHURCH, LISTEN TO MAN'S VOICE AND NOT MY VOICE.

I AM A JEALOUS GOD.

I HAVE SEEN EVERYTHING.

I know EVERY SINGLE DECISION THAT HAS BEEN MADE by every single one of my shepherds across the earth, who I HAVE ENTRUSTED to care for my sheep.

I have ALLOWED for the world to see that my church has allowed itself to BOW DOWN TO THE FEAR OF MAN, and to not be living with THE REVERENT FEAR OF ME, the

Lord of lords, the King of kings, the One who created all life, THE ONE WHO SUSTAINS ALL LIFE, but EVERYTHING THAT HAS BEEN TAKING PLACE IS ALL A PART OF MY DIVINE WILL, FOR I AM SOVEREIGN, and one by one, I have been coming down from heaven, mounted on a mighty angelic being, to rescue my chosen people. To pull my chosen people out of the DARKNESS, out of the MIRY CLAY, out of the DEEP WATERS, and I have been SETTING THEM ON FIRE, and their freedom comes through me the Lord of lords and THROUGH ME ALONE.

I HAVE BEEN SETTING MY PEOPLE ON FIRE, and you my shepherd, you are a shepherd of my sheep, AND I WILL NO LONGER TOLERATE MY SHEEP BEING TAUGHT A WATERED-DOWN GOSPEL.

I WILL NO LONGER TOLERATE my sheep being taught to allow the FEAR OF MAN to influence their decisions.

I WILL NO LONGER TOLERATE my shepherds LEADING MY FLOCK ASTRAY.

I WILL NO LONGER TOLERATE my shepherds not instilling the REVERENT FEAR OF ME into the hearts, minds, bodies, souls and spirits of my sheep.

I WILL NO LONGER TOLERATE my shepherds BOWING DOWN TO MAN.

MY JUDGEMENT IS COMING UPON MY CHURCH.

MY JUDGEMENT IS COMING UPON EVERYONE WITHIN A POSITION OF INFLUENCE WITHIN MY CHURCH, and I AM a jealous God. I AM a devouring fire, and I WILL NO LONGER TOLERATE MY SHEPHERDS BEING LUKEWARM.

I WILL NO LONGER TOLERATE my shepherds leading a flock who are lukewarm, FOR IF ANYONE IS LUKEWARM, NEITHER COLD NOT HOT, I WILL VOMIT THEM OUT OF MY MOUTH.

My beloved shepherd, my Spirit is bringing conviction upon you now of WHERE YOU HAVE SINNED. My Spirit is bringing conviction upon you now of WHAT YOU NEED TO REPENT FOR, and it is by my Spirit that I will convict you of WHAT MESSAGES YOU NEED TO GIVE TO MY SHEEP.

I have called you by name from your mother's womb to RAISE UP MY PEOPLE who live with the REVERENT FEAR OF ME the Lord their God.

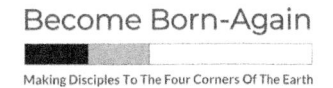

You know that my Word tells you and all my people who have the eyes to see and the ears to hear, that as you go, proclaim this message, "The Kingdom of Heaven has come near. Heal the sick, raise the dead, cleanse those who have leprosy, drive out demons. Freely you have received, freely give."

MY WORD tells my people that they can do ALL THINGS through me, the Lord who strengthens them.

MY WORD tells my people that they are to WALK WORTHY OF THE CALLING with which they are called.

MY WORD tells my people that whoever confesses Me before men, him I will also confess before My Father who is in heaven, put whoever denies Me before men, him I will also deny before my Father who is in heaven.

MY WORD tells my people to remember that IT IS A SIN to know what you ought to do and then not do it.

MY WORD tells my people that whoever wants to be my disciple MUST DENY THEMSELVES and take up their cross DAILY and follow Me, for WHOEVER WANTS TO SAVE THEIR LIFE WILL LOSE IT, but whoever loses their life for me will save it.

MY WORD tells my people that "You are of God, little children, and have overcome them, because He who is in you is greater than he who is in the world", and MY WORD tells you my shepherd and all my sheep, "You are the light of the world. A town built on a hill cannot be hidden. Neither do people light a lamp and put it under a bowl. Instead they put it on its stand and it gives light to everyone in the house. In the same way, LET YOUR LIGHT SHINE before others that they may SEE YOUR GOOD DEEDS and GLORIFY YOUR FATHER IN HEAVEN".

My beloved shepherd, I AM SETTING A FIRE INSIDE OF YOU… A FIRE THAT WILL NEVER GO OUT.

I have ANOINTED your head with oil.

As you are receiving my words now I am releasing an ANOINTING OF MY SPIRIT AND OF POWER INTO YOUR LIFE.

NEVER AGAIN WILL YOU PREACH A WATERED-DOWN GOSPEL.

NEVERY AGAIN WILL YOU LEAD ANY OF MY FLOCK ASTRAY.

NEVER AGAIN WILL YOU ALLOW THE FEAR OF MAN TO BE ON ANY OF YOUR CONGREGATION.

NEVER AGAIN WILL YOU TOLERATE THE SINS THAT YOU HAVE TOLERATED.

NEVER AGAIN WILL YOU BE SELECTIVE IN YOUR OWN SIN.

My Word tells you that YOU ARE TO BE HOLY, JUST AS I AM HOLY.

My beloved shepherd, the sheep that I have entrusted you with and my sheep that I am going to be bringing to hear your messages, from me through your tongue, YOU ARE GOING TO BE RELEASING ANOINTINGS INTO THEIR LIFE.

I am going to be USING YOU to set them on fire, for my Word tells you and all my people that "Everyone who calls on my name will be saved. But how can they call on me to save them unless they believe in me? And how can they believe in me, if they have never heard about me? And how can they hear about me, unless someone tells them, and how will anyone go and tell them without being sent? That is why the Scriptures say "How beautiful are the feet of messengers who bring good news.""

My beloved shepherd, NO LONGER AM I GOING TO TOLERATE MY CHURCH BEING WITHIN THE FOUR WALLS, for my church is across the entire Earth, and my beloved shepherd, YOU ARE RESPONSIBLE FOR PREACHING THE PURE GOSPEL.

YOU ARE RESPONSIBLE FOR PREACHING ABOUT THE POWER OF MY SPIRIT.

YOU ARE RESPONSIBLE FOR PREACHING ABOUT DELIVERANCE FROM DEMONIC OPPRESSION.

YOU ARE RESPONSIBLE FOR INSTILLING A FIRE INSIDE OF YOUR CONGREGATION, SO THAT THEY START TO BECOME MY HANDS AND FEET.

YOU ARE RESPONSIBLE FOR ENSURING THAT EVERYONE WHO LISTENS TO YOUR MESSAGES, which will be the messages that I will give you by my Spirit, THEY WILL NOT BE VOMITED OUT OF MY MOUTH FOR BEING LUKEWARM.

I the Sovereign Lord are beginning to SET MY CHURCH ON FIRE, and there is NOTHING ANYONE IN ANY POSITION OF POWER OR CONTROL OR EARTHLY WEALTH CAN DO ABOUT IT.

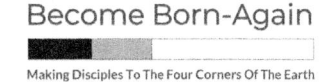

MY KINGDOM COME, MY WILL BE DONE, IN EARTH AS IT IS IN HEAVEN.

REVELATION

God is going to give you revelation about your life & the world He created

But you are not like that, for you are a chosen people. You are royal priests, a holy nation, God's very own possession.

As a result, you can show others the goodness of God, for he called you out of the darkness into his wonderful light.

1 Peter 2:9

So all of us who have had that veil removed can see and reflect the glory of the Lord. And the Lord—who is the Spirit—makes us more and more like him as we are changed into his glorious image.

2 Corinthians 3:18

30th September 2022

I Am Revealing To You What Is The Purpose Of Your Life Here On Earth, Says The Lord

My beloved, you are receiving my message to you now, for it is written, it was ordained, before I created the heavens and the earth.

I am revealing to you what is the purpose of your life here on earth.

Before I lifted the veil for you, before I removed the scales from your eyes, before I gave you the eyes to see and the ears to hear, before I began softening your hardened heart, you lived on earth often striving to have meaning in your life, desiring to have a purpose in life.

My beloved, you have been through many things in your life. You have experienced things in your life that many, many other people walking the earth would not have survived. At times, you have felt totally and completely lost. At times you have been completely overwhelmed with fear. You have been in some very dark valleys. You have had times in your life when you felt completely surrounded. So surrounded that no matter which way you turned, no matter what you said, no matter what you did, no matter what you tried to do to break out of that situation, you were continually being attacked by people in your life, by your circumstances, by financial challenges, by health issues.

You have had people during your life telling you what is the best thing to do. What is the right thing to do. You have been confused. You have felt something on your heart, yet people in your life have said different. In your life when you have hit a crossroads, you have sometimes been like a rabbit in the headlights, not knowing which way to turn.

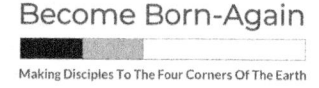

My beloved, from when I created you, from when I formed you, from when I knitted you together in utter seclusion, from when I brought you forth on the day you were born at the exact time and the exact place where you came into a world, I the Lord have been with you. I the Lord have carried you. I the Lord have sustained you. Yes, I have ALWAYS sustained your life, and I will ALWAYS continue to sustain your life, because my beloved, YOU ARE CHOSEN AND NOT FORSAKEN.

I have called you by name from your mother's womb to have the purpose and the calling that I am revealing to you in my message here.

Your purpose that you are going to be living out for the rest of your life on earth, IS TO BE MY GLORY CARRIER.

You may be wondering "what does it mean to be your glory carrier?".

My beautiful, fearfully and wonderfully made child, let me explain.

Firstly, your identity is not in the things that you have experienced during your life.

Your identity is not in your family.

Your identity is not in the experiences that you've had.

Your identity is not in what people have said about you.

Your identity is not in how people have treated you.

Your identity is not in your appearance.

My beloved, YOUR IDENTITY IS IN ME THE LORD YOUR GOD AND IN ME ALONE.

I have poured my spirit in to you, and greater is the spirit that is in you than the spirit that is in the world. My beloved, YOU CAN DO AND YOU WILL DO ALL THINGS THROUGH ME the Lord your God who gives you strength.

By you following the two greatest commandments, by my spirit, your purpose to be my glory carrier is going to become absolutely natural for you.

Being my glory carrier means that you seek my kingdom and my righteousness first at the start of every single day, and my promise to you is all else will be given unto you.

BEING MY GLORY CARRIER MEANS BEING MY HANDS AND FEET.

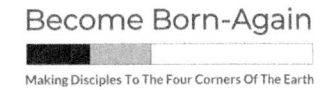

As you receive my words now, I am releasing the gift of faith. I am releasing the gift of tongues. I am releasing the gift of prophecy. I am releasing the gift of healing. Yes, my beloved, by faith as you receive everything that I'm pouring into you now, I am equipping you to truly, truly, truly live the rest of your life as my glory carrier.

From this moment going forward, following you receiving my message to you, where I have given you, I have put inside of you, your purpose on earth for the rest of your life, you will begin to experience life going from glory to glory to glory.

By the power of my spirit, I have now DESTROYED every yoke of bondage that has been in place, that has kept you in a place of waiting. I am RELEASING into your life right now an outpouring of my spirit. You are being filled with my spirit now.

MY FIRE, MY DEVOURING FIRE, IS FALLING UPON YOU NOW.

Raise your arms to the air. Praise me. Worship Me. Thank me. Glorify glorify glorify your Father in heaven.

From this moment forward, by you following the two greatest commandments, the first to love me with all your heart, with all your mind, with all your soul, with all your strength, and secondly, to love your neighbour as yourself, YOU WILL NOW BE HEARING MY VOICE THROUGHOUT EVERY DAY.

I have given you the ears to hear my voice and to know my voice.

I will speak to you to guide your steps through each day.

I will speak to you to give you wisdom, understanding and revelation.

I will speak to you to give you clarity and to remove any possible confusion.

I will speak to you to tell you how proud I am of you.

I will speak to you and say "keep trusting me, keep trusting me"

I will speak to you and say "keep your eyes focused on me".

I will speak to you and I will say "remember that I am working in ALL THINGS FOR GOOD".

I will speak to you through my Word in ways in which you have never experienced before. You are going to be gaining wisdom, understanding and deep revelation through my Word in ways in which you have never experienced before.

My beloved, live your life worthy of the calling that you have received, of the purpose that I have put inside of you.

You are chosen.

You are ordained.

You are anointed.

You are fearfully and wonderfully made in my image.

You have received all the spiritual gifts that you need to do everything that I have ordained for the rest of your life.

It is not you that live, but I that live in you.

You will never again hide your light under a bushel.

My beloved, YOU ARE MY GLORY CARRIER, and the world is going to see that you are my hands and feet, says I, the Sovereign Lord.

May 5th 2023

Your 3 Years Of Preparation Has Come To An End, Says The Lord

My beloved child, it has been three years.

Since the beginning of the year 2020, it has been three years.

It has been three years that you have been in the REFINERS FIRE.

It has been three years that I have sent the LOCUSTS into your life.

It has been three years that I have been SANCTIFYING YOU.

I has been three years that I have been PURIFYING YOU.

It has been three years that I have been building your faith in me, the Lord your God.

It has been three years that I have been STRAIGHTENING OUT your crooked paths.

It has been three years that I have been TEACHING YOU TO DISCERN WHAT IS FROM ME and what is not from me.

It has been three years that I have been SEPARATING YOU out from the things of the world.

It has been three years that I have been showing you that your TRUST has to be in me, the Lord your God, and me alone.

It has been three years that I have been completely TRANSFORMING THE PEOPLE that are in your life, that speak into your life.

It has been three years that I have been PREPARING YOU to receive my words now.

It has been three years that I have increasingly been SPEAKING TO YOU through my Word, which is ALIVE AND ACTIVE.

It has been three years that I have had you on the POTTER'S WHEEL, for I am the potter and you are the clay.

It has been three years that I the Lord have been DESTROYING in you your OLD WINESKINS.

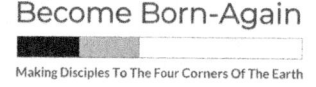

It has been three years that I have been TRANSFORMING THE WAY YOU THINK, FEEL AND ACT EACH DAY.

It has been three years that I have allowed the enemy to at times RELENTLESSLY TRY TO KILL YOU.

It has been three years where you have had times when you have been SURROUNDED ON ALL SIDES BY YOUR ENEMIES.

It has been three years that I have been transforming the way you think by the RENEWAL OF YOUR MIND.

It has been three years that I have been EQUIPPING YOU YOU TO TRULY BECOME ONE OF MY DISCIPLES.

It has been three years that I have been TRAINING YOU TO BE MY HANDS AND FEET UPON THE EARTH.

It has been three years that I have only just begun GIVING YOU GLIMPSES OF MY GLORY.

It has been three years where I have only just begun giving you DIVINE ENCOUNTERS IN YOUR DAY TO DAY LIFE.

It has been three years that I have been preparing for A FIRE TO RISE UP ON THE INSIDE OF YOU THAT WILL NEVER GO OUT.

It has been three years that you have been experiencing and witnessing me once again SHAKE THE HEAVENS AND THE EARTH.

It has been three years that you have seen me, the Lord your God, EXPOSE THE SINS OF THE WORLD.

It has been three years that you have been living in and through me beginning to bring in a NEW AGE.

It has been three years that you have seen me begin MY SEPARATION.

My beloved child, it has been three years of PREPARATION FOR YOU TO BECOME TRULY MY HANDS AND FEET.

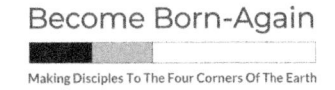

I have put my Spirit into YOU, and greater is the Spirit that is in you that the spirit that is in the world.

The SAME POWER that raised me from the dead LIVES IN YOU.

NO LONGER WILL YOU IN ANY WAY HOLD BACK from telling people whom you have never met before about me.

For you know that everyone who calls on my name will be saved, but how can people call on me to save them unless they believe in me? And how can they believe in me if they have never heard about me? And how can they hear about me unless someone tells them? And how will anyone go and tell them without being sent?

My beloved child, I have CALLED YOU BY NAME from your mother's womb to go to TELL PEOPLE ABOUT ME.

For the rest of your life I am going to be sending you out as ONE OF MY DISCIPLES.

Yes, my beloved child, you are my hands and feet, and YOU WILL DO the same things that I have done and EVEN GREATER THINGS. You will be able to say to ANY MOUNTAIN may you be lifted up and thrown into the sea, and because you have faith, BECAUSE YOU HAVE MY FAITH, and do not doubt, IT WILL HAPPEN.

For the rest of your life, when you hear me say "Who can I send as a messenger to my lost sheep? Who will go for me?" my beloved child, you will say "HERE I AM. SEND ME."

My beloved child, it is not by your strength, it is not by your might, but it is by my Spirit that you will LIVE YOUR LIFE WORTHY OF THE CALLING THAT YOU HAVE RECEIVED.

YOUR THREE YEARS OF PREPARATION HAS COME TO AN END. Now it is time to go and be my hands and feet, says I, the Sovereign Lord.

June 11th 2022

My Beloved, Let Tears Flow & Open Your Heart To Me, Says The Lord

My beloved, you are my masterpiece. Before I created the heavens and the earth, every single day of your life was written in my book. Every single moment, every single tear, was laid out before a single day had passed.

You are my masterpiece. I formed you, I created you, I knitted you together in utter seclusion. I brought you forth on the day you were born. It has been I the Lord your God that have carried you through every single trial, tribulation, storm and period of pain and suffering that you have ever experienced.

It is only I the Lord your God that true truly know what you have been through.

It is only I the Lord your God that have heard what people have said about you.

It is only I the Lord your God have known every single thought that you have ever had.

It is only I the Lord your God that know the shame, the guilt, the fear, the condemnation, the anger, the bitterness, the rage, the unforgiveness, the battles that you have gone through. My beloved, the battle belongs to me, the Lord your God.

My beloved, let the tears flow. My beloved, open your heart to me. Let tears gush from your eyes. No longer hold back the tears. My beloved the tears that you are shedding, tears that you will shed from this moment forward from you receiving my message to you, your tears are no longer tears of sorrow, tears of shame, tears of guilt, tears of fear, tears of feeling helpless, tears of feeling hopeless. My beloved, your tears are tears of breakthrough. Your tears are tears of knowing that you are loved by me beyond anything that you can comprehend.

My beloved, my plans for your life are plans for good and not for disaster to give you a future and a hope. Every single tear that you shed, I catch them in my bottle, and because you plant in tears you will harvest with shouts of joy.

I the Lord your God, I am the one that saves you from death. I save your eyes from tears and your feet from stumbling. Through you pouring out feelings and emotions from your past life experiences, you are going to be experiencing breakthrough, you are going to be experiencing sudden transformations in how you think, feel and act.

My beloved, let the tears flow. My beloved, raise your arms to the air as the tears are flowing. Embrace the tears. My beloved, your eyes, where your tears come from, have not seen, your ears have not heard and your mind has not yet conceived what I the Lord your God have got planned for you because you love me.

You are my masterpiece, and my plans for your life are plans for good and not for disaster to give you a future and a hope.

January 20th 2022

Let The Tears Flow, I Am Breaking Generational Curses Now, Says The Lord

My beloved child, I have seen every tear that you have ever shed. I have captured them in my bottle, and because you have sown with tears you are going to reap with joy. Yes, for I the Lord your God have spoken, I am bringing you my joy, yes, my joy, I am bringing you the fruit of the Spirit, love, joy, peace, patience, forgiveness, long-suffering, self-control, goodness, gratefulness. Yes, yes. The fruit of the Spirit is your portion. I am going to be leading you into tears of joy. You will be weeping tears of joy as I move in your life like I have never moved before. Because I the Lord your God had been refining you by fire. I have been creating in you new wineskins, your old self, your old habits, behaviours, thoughts, feelings, emotions, those feelings of guilt, shame, condemnation, anger, bitterness, rage, unforgiveness, anxiety, depression, fear. These are all your old wineskins and I do not pour my new wine into your old wineskins because your old wineskins, your old self, would burst under the pressure, spilling the new wine and ruining your old wineskins. But no, instead I have been refining you by fire. You have been going through the refiner's fire. Yes, the refiners fire. Every single thing that you have been through I have allowed you to go through because I have brought you to this moment right now for me to speak into your heart, for you to know that you are fearfully and wonderfully made. I have been refining you by fire. You have been in the refiner's fire, and you have not been burnt up just like Shadrach, Meshach and Abednego because I the Lord your God had been in there with you. Yes, I have been in there with you. You have been refined seven times over your identity is no in me. Your identity is in me and in me alone. And now I have been preparing you and I am now ready to pour into your life my new wine, my new glory, my new love, my new peace, my new joy, more patience. Yes, I am giving you more patience. I am giving you wisdom and discernment like you have never had before. Yes, I the Lord your God are giving you wisdom, wisdom from my word, wisdom through my Holy Spirit, wisdom that you have never had before. And you will never again fear man. You will never again trust in anyone who will be deceiving you because my spirit is upon you, and my Spirit will convict you. When someone is trying to lie to you when you are seeing a headline, a video, something on the radio, anything that comes into your ear gates or eye gates that is a lie that is a deception, my spirit will convict you and show you and I will say no, that is a lie. Because my holy spirit guides you into all truth.

And I say to you now let the tears flow, the tears of joy let them flow. I am immersing you now in My Holy Spirit, I am pouring into your life my rivers of living waters. The dry wastelands of your life they are gushing now with my living waters. Right now in your life, the dry bones those that have been dried, buried bones, the dead is been brought to life, the dry bones in your life are rattling now, for I the Lord your God have spoken. The dry bones are coming alive and I the Lord your God, I am putting skin and sinew onto these dry bones. The dry bones in your life and your circumstances, your finances, your family, your loved ones, your health, your mental health, your physical health, your job, everything in your life, everything that has been dry, everything that has been dead and buried, I am speaking life into those dry bones now and those dry bones are coming alive, and the people in your life are going to know that I the Lord your God, I am the Lord of Heaven's armies, I am the King of kings, The Lord of Lords, the name above all names. I am the way, the truth and the life. I am the good shepherd, I am the gate, I am the bread of life, I am the true vine, I am the King of glory. I am the King of glory. Yes, I am the King of glory.

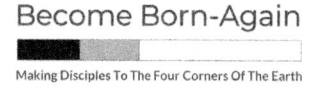

I am the way, the truth and the Life, I am the resurrection and the life and I have called you out of the darkness into my glorious light, and you are a glory carrier for me. Yes, you are a glory carrier for me says I the Lord your God. I am your Lord and Saviour. I reached down to the bottom of the deepest, darkest ocean to rescue you, to pull you out, out of that miry clay and I have put your feet on me the rock of God, the rock of all ages. You are mine, says the Lord, you are mine. I have anointed your head with oil. My hand is mighty upon you. And you from this moment forward will be walking by faith, not by sight. You from this moment forward will be devouring my word, because your faith comes from hearing and hearing by my word. You will stand on this word, you will listen back to this word and this word that you are hearing from me now will lead you into floods of tears, because you know, because I have put my spirit in you, that this is me the Lord your God speaking to you right now. I am transforming you, healing you, redeeming you, setting you free, I am breaking the iron chains of bondage, I am breaking off you now your addictions. Any remaining addictions in your life I am breaking them off now in my name, by my blood for I the Lord your God have spoken. The chains of bondage in your life, the generational curses in your life, the ancestral curses in your life are breaking now in my name. I am the chain breaker. Yes, I am the chain breaker. I am the King of glory. My name is a name above all names. Every knee bows in my name, in my presence. The demons are fleeing now. The enemies are fleeing from your life now. The demonic strongholds, the powers and principalities, the generational curses, the ancestral curses, they are all breaking now in my name. The strongmen that have been upon your life and your family are being destroyed now in my name, for I the Lord your God have spoken.

And in this place, I bring peace. In this place, I bring peace. The peace I give you is a gift the world cannot give you. You are so precious in my eyes. You are the apple of my eye. Peace, be still. Peace, be still.

April 25th 2022

I Am Fully Healing You From All Your Life Traumas, Says The Lord

My beloved, this is the Lord your God. I have called you by name. I rescued you from all your enemies. Before I created the heavens and the earth, every day of your life was written in my book, every moment was laid out before a single day had passed.

You have been through and experienced trials and tribulations, hurt and turmoil that many, many other people would not have come through, they would not have survived. But you have come through everything that I have allowed you to go through, for this time that you are living in now. I am for you and not against you and my hand has been upon your life through every single moment, through everything that you have experienced, through every dark valley that you have been in. It has been I the Lord your God that has carried you.

I know that one of the most challenging things for you to do is to praise me and to worship me and to thank me and to glorify me in the challenging times, in the dark times, in the valleys. For my Sons and Daughters currently experiencing trials and tribulations, some of you more than you have experienced in your life before, some of you due to an accumulation of your life experiences, you have been living without my joy. You have been living without my peace. You have been living with pains from your past, you have been living with the trauma of the things that you have experienced, things that you have lived through, how people have treated you, the things that have come against you. But my message to you my beloved Sons and Daughters, is that my plans for your life, are plans for good and not for disaster to give you a future and a hope, and I am calling you to embrace that you are where you are in your life right now, because of every single moment of your entire life.

I am calling you to come to this place of knowing that everything that you have ever experienced was always a part of my divine plan for your life. I have allowed you to experience things which most other people walking the earth have never experienced, but through you coming into a place of being joyful and thankful of the breath in your lungs, of being joyful and thankful that I the Lord your God have carried you through every single moment of your life, no matter how deep, no matter how dark, no matter how many locusts have come into your life and that have stripped you down or that have stripped you bear, no matter how many tears that you have ever shed, I have caught every one of your tears in my bottle, and because you have sown with tears you are going to reap with joy.

My heart for you my beloved Sons and Daughters is that you come more and more into my presence, to see more of your life through my eyes, because you are the apple of my eye, you are my masterpiece, and I have got great plans for your life. I have anointed you. I have made a way where there seems no way. During your life I have closed doors that no man can open and right now I am opening doors in your life that no man can shut. So my beloved Sons and Daughters, I am calling you to let all your inhibitions go, to be willing to praise me and worship me in spirit and in truth in spite of the things that you have experienced.

My beloved, there have been chains that have been still keeping you held back to experiences that you have had in your life. And some of these chains have seemed unbreakable. Some of these chains have seemed so heavy that they will never be broken. But my word to you right now is that I am the chain breaker. I am the way maker. Every chain breaks in my name. I am releasing upon you now my beloved Sons and Daughters, a destroyer anointing. I am destroying what have been the remaining chains that have held you captive, that have stolen your joy because I am now bringing you into a place where you will be experiencing my joy and my peace which surpasses all understanding. You will be experiencing these things each day that you will be glorifying me, testifying of my goodness, of my unfailing love, of my grace, of my mercy, of my miracle saving powers, of how I have saved you and rescued you from all your enemies, because you my beloved Sons and Daughters, you are my chosen people, and no weapons formed against you have ever prospered and no weapons that would be formed against you moving forward will prosper, and every tongue that rises up against you, you will condemn because this is the heritage of me the Lord your God. You are cleansed by my blood. You are protected by my hand. I have put my spirit in you in the spirit that is in you is greater than the spirit that is in the world.

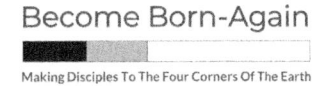

You are fearfully and wonderfully made. In my image. My beloved let go of the pains of your past. Let go of the things that I have allowed you to go through that have tormented you. The things which have stolen your peace and your joy, no more, says I, the Lord of Heavens Armies.

My beloved Sons and Daughters through you lifting your arms to the air, through you surrendering everything to me, through your pure hearts and your clean hands, you will see me move so mightily in your life, unlike you have ever experienced before. Your eyes haven't seen and your ears haven't heard and your mind hasn't conceived what I the Lord your God have got planned for you, because you love me, because you trust in me, because you know that in spite of every single trial, tribulation, pain, turmoil and grief that you have experienced in your life, I the Lord your God work in all things in your life for good, because you love me and because you live according to my purpose for you.

My way is perfect. I have called you by name to be my glory carrier, and my peace which surpasses all understanding will guard your heart and your mind in me, the Lord your God.

My peace is a gift to you that the world cannot give you, and I am now loosening an anointing of power and authority upon you in the spirit realm unlike you have ever had before. Throughout your entire life, I have made a table for you in the presence of your enemies, but, you are mine. You are no longer a slave to your sin nature. No weapons formed against you will ever prosper. I have called you by name to be my glory carrier, to walk in truth, in victory, with my love, with my peace, with my authority in the spiritual realm.

Remember my beloved Sons and Daughters, greater is a spirit that is in you than the spirit that is in the world. You have no fear because my perfect love expels all fear, and when I send my word out into your life, it does not return to me void, it accomplishes all that I desire and it prospers everywhere that I'm sending it now., deep into your heart, your mind, your body and your spirit.

You are my masterpiece, says I the Lord of Heaven's Armies.

November 18th 2022

I Am Doing A Miracle Heart Transplant In You, Says The Lord

My beloved precious child, I have seen everything that you have been through during your life. I have seen how people have treated you. I have seen every painful and every traumatic experience that you've had. I know the times when you have felt helpless. I know the times when you have felt hopeless. I know when you have been crushed in spirit. I have seen every tear that you've ever shed. It is I the Lord your God that have carried you in my arms through every one of the dark valleys you have been through.

It is I the Lord your God that gave you the strength to come through those experiences in your life that many other people walking the earth would not have survived.

My beloved child, I have called you by name from your mother's womb. You are chosen and not forsaken. I am for you and not against you. I have plans for your life, plans for good and not for disaster to give you a future and a hope.

What I the Lord are doing inside of you, as you are receiving my words now, I am doing a miracle heart transplant. The heart that you were born with has become a stony heart due to everything that you have experienced during your life. The pain, the suffering, the heartache, how other people have treated you.

My beloved I want you to now imagine the heart inside of you. This heart of stone, and all around your heart of stone are chains, and these are chains to your past. These are chains to your past life experiences, for it is your past life experiences that have led to your heart becoming hardened and becoming stubborn and stony, but as you imagine now your stony heart wrapped in impenetrable chains without a way to unlock, also imagine that around your hardened heart wrapped in chains are iron bars all around, like prison bars. What appear to be impenetrable iron bars. This is how you have been living and experiencing life with your hardened heart in chains to your past, behind an impenetrable prison and iron bars.

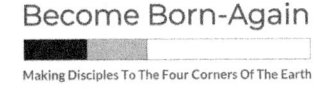

What I the Lord are doing now on the inside of you, as you receive my words, as I am pouring my Spirit into you, I am destroying every one of those iron bars.

They are destroyed now.

I am destroying every single chain now, for every chain breaks in my name, and now with just your hardened heart of stone visible, I the Lord your God, I am now taking out of you your heart of stone and giving you a new heart, a responsive heart, a tender heart of flesh, and with your new heart of flesh, for the first time in your life, not only will you begin to truly love me with all your heart, with all your mind, with all your soul with all your strength, but you will also truly be able to love your neighbour as yourself, including those people that have hurt you the most in your life.

My beloved child, as you lay at the foot of my cross your unforgiveness, as I am pouring my Spirit into you, I am going to give you the strength now to not only confess with your tongue, with all your heart, that you forgive those who have hurt you during your life, by my Spirit, you will also be able to pray and ask me to set them free from their life that is dominated by sin, by darkness, by acts of evil.

Thank you, my beloved child, for receiving my message. Thank you my beloved child for receiving by faith, your new heart of flesh, from your old heart of stone, for when I send my Word out into your life and into the lives of my people across the earth, it does not return to me void, it accomplishes all that I desire and it prospers everywhere that I send it.

My beloved child, fix your eyes on me. I am the author and the finisher of your faith. I am your strength. I am your hope. You get your peace from me, and the peace that I give you is a gift the world cannot give you.

Go forth, my beloved, fearfully and wonderfully made child. I have called you by name from your mother's womb to be my glory carrier, to be my hands and feet, says I the Sovereign Lord.

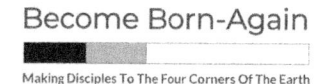

December 9th 2022

You Are Not In A Battle, You Are IN ME, Says The Lord

My beloved child, I am calling you now to no longer see yourself in a battle.

My desire is for you to no longer say "I am in a battle with the enemy" because my beloved, you are in ME. Your identity is IN ME and IN ME alone. I have put my Spirit into you, and greater is the spirit that is in you than the spirit that is in the world.

I have made you the head and NOT the tail.

I have made a table for you in the presence of your enemies, but your enemies FLEE when you use and you stand on the authority that I have given you, your authority that is IN ME, the King of kings, the Lord of lords, the one given the name above ALL names.

My desire is for you to live in joy and peace EVERY DAY.

My beloved child, cast ALL your burdens upon me because I care for you, for my yoke is easy and my burden is light.

I desire for you to be content in ALL circumstances, no matter where you are at any given moment, because remember my beloved, every day of your life is written in my book. Every single moment, including this moment right now as you receive my words to you, was laid out before a single day had passed, and my plans for you, my beloved child, are plans for good and not for disaster to give you a future and a hope.

My hand is mighty upon you. No weapons formed against you will ever prosper, and every tongue that rises up against you, you will condemn for that is a heritage of the servants of me, the Lord your God.

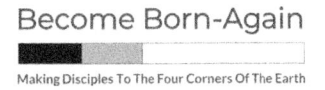

I have not given you a spirit of fear, but of power, of love and a sound mind. As you are receiving my words to you now, I am pouring my Spirit into you. My devouring fire has destroyed the remaining yolks of bondage in your life. I have put my Spirit into you, and I have given you a new heart, a heart of flesh from the heart of stone you once lived with.

Remember, the two most important commandments are first to love me with all your heart, with all your mind, with all your soul and with all your strength, and secondly, to love your neighbour as yourself.

Remember my beloved, for the rest of your life, you are NOT in a battle with the enemy, YOU ARE IN ME. Your help comes from me, the Lord, the Creator of the heavens and the earth.

I the Lord your God, the Alpha and the Omega, the beginning and the end, the first and the last, I am for you and not against you, and because I am for you, my beloved, who can EVER be against you?

You are IN ME NOW, and you will always be IN ME, says I the Sovereign Lord.

May 30th 2022

My Beloved, Please Don't Compare Yourself Anymore To Anyone Else, Says The Lord

My beloved, many are called, but few are chosen. I have called you by name. I have chosen you. My beloved, you are chosen and not forsaken. My beloved, my desire for you is that YOU WILL NO LONGER COMPARE YOURSELF TO ANYONE ELSE. The days of you living feeling inferior to others is over, says I the Lord of Heaven Armies.

I meet you where you are. You are fearfully and wonderfully made in my image.

My beloved, you are the apple of my eye.

Your identity is in me the Lord your God, and in me alone.

Your identity is not in your circumstances.

Your identity is not in your childhood experiences.

Your identity is not in your family.

Your identity is not in the relationships that you have had.

Your identity is not in the sins of your past.

Your identity is not in what anyone has ever told you about yourself.

Your identity, my beloved, is in me the Lord your God, and in me alone.

I have seen how you have felt when you have compared yourself to others.

I have seen when you have felt inferior.

I have seen when you have desired to have what other people have.

I have seen when you have been striving to attain what others have achieved.

I have seen when you have been envious of other people.

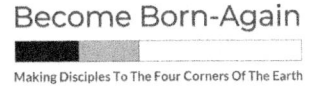

I have seen when you have looked upon others and thought "I want what they have", but my beloved, remember, the first will be last and the last will be first.

My plans for your life, my beloved, are plans for good and not for disaster to give you a future and a hope.

Put your complete trust in me. Do not be afraid. Lean not on your own understanding.

My beloved, my plans for your life, yes your life, are plans for good and not for disaster to give you a future and a hope. I have called you by name to be my glory carrier, and I use broken people like you and everyone that is in your life, to rescue broken people like you and everyone in your life.

I am the one that turns your ashes into beauty.

I am the one that brings you hope.

I am the one that gives you a heart of flesh, from a heart of stone.

I am the one that takes away all the pain and suffering and trauma and guilt and shame and condemnation from your life experiences.

I am the one who gives you life.

Your identity is in me, and in me alone.

My beloved, you can do ALL THINGS through me the Lord your God who gives you strength.

My beloved, before I created the heavens and the earth, I planned for this moment right now, for you to be receiving my words to you. May you never, ever again compare yourself to anyone that is in your life and that will come into your life in future.

As I the Lord your God bring more brothers and sisters into your life, do not compare yourself to them. Each of them are following what I laid out in my book, because remember my beloved, every moment of your entire life and the lives of every man, woman and child walking the earth and that will walk the earth, every moment of your lives was laid out before a single day had passed.

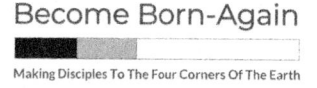

My beloved, you, are the apple of my eye.

You are my masterpiece.

I have called you by name to be my glory carrier, and as you saturate yourself with the things of my Kingdom, as you read my Word, as you hear my Word, as you listen to anointed worship music, as you spend time in fellowship with your brothers and your sisters, as you switch off and turn away from the things of this world and instead you focus on the things above, not the things below, as you saturate yourself with my Kingdom, my beloved, my promise to you is that I will be saturating you with my glory.

So you, my beloved, are going to go from glory to glory to glory, says I, the Lord of Heaven's Armies.

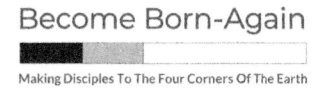

August 18th 2022

I Am Asking You To Completely Surrender & Let Go Of Those Things In Your Life You Have Been Fighting For, Says The Lord

My beloved, I am asking you to completely surrender and let go of those things in your life that you have been fighting for.

Trust me. Trust my Word. Trust in my promises to you.

Lean not on your own understanding.

It will seem almost impossible for you to completely surrender and let go, because you will feel like this is meaning that you are giving up. The truth is, through your complete surrender and letting go, you will be putting your total and complete trust in me and in me alone.

Remember my beloved, my thoughts are nothing like your thoughts, and my ways are far beyond anything you could imagine. For just as the heavens are higher than the earth, so my ways are higher than your ways and my thoughts higher than your thoughts.

My beloved, I want you to rest in and experience my peace which surpasses all understanding. I want you to experience joy. I want you to live each day by faith and not by sight.

My beloved, as you are receiving my words to you now, by my Spirit, I am revealing to you what you need to surrender and let go of. Give up ALL control.

You have shown me how you desire to serve me, to worship me, to have your faith in me, and now through you completely trusting that I have heard every one of your prayers for those things which you have carried, for those battles that you have been in, you will realise that my yoke is easy and my burden is light.

My beloved, your eyes haven't seen, your ears haven't heard and your mind hasn't conceived what I the Lord your God have got planned for you, because you love me.

Let go and let me bring you into tears of total and utter joy, as I do in your life, what no man can do, says I, the Lord your God.

February 2nd 2022

I Meet You Wherever You Are. I Have Always Loved You And I Will Always Love You, Says The Lord

My beloved, you haven't yet accepted me into your life as your Lord and Saviour, but I am patient and I love you, and I have always been faithful to you, and I will always be faithful.

I know the reasons why you haven't turned to me. I know every one of your life experiences, of your pains, of your emotions, which has led you to a place of not believing in me, not seeking me. I the Lord your God meet you wherever you are. Some of you are in a place in your life where things are good. You have a stable job. You have a stable income. You have your home, you have your family, and often during your life, you have thought to yourself that you don't need me in your life if I am real.

I meet you wherever you are. I meet you and your family wherever you all are. You may not be broken-hearted and crushed in spirit, and my desire for you is that you don't need to get to that place to turn to Me, the Lord your God, and to receive me into your life as your Lord and Saviour.

I love you with my unfailing love. I know everything about you. I formed you, I created you, I knitted you together in utter seclusion in your mother's womb. I have numbered every hair on your head. My thoughts for you, my beloved, outnumber the grains of sand on the seashore. I will never stop loving you. I know what you are going to say even before you say it.

I have been with you through every moment of your entire life. In the most challenging, darkest periods of your life, in your periods of grief through the loss of a loved one, it has been by the Lord your God that have carried you in my arms. It is I the Lord your God that has given you the strength to come through the battles, the trials and the tribulations of your life.

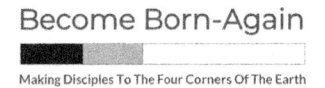

I the Lord your God have been misrepresented in the world. There has been so many lies, so much deception, so much corruption and my church too hasn't been representing me truthfully. My beloved, it is right for you to not want anything to do with religion. Man-made religion causes division. Man-made religion can lead to the devastation of human life. I am calling you, my beloved, into a personal relationship with me the Lord your God. You have always been in the palm of my hand and you will always be in the palm of my hand. I will never stop loving you. I cannot deny who I am, and throughout your life, my mercy and my grace has been upon you. It is I the Lord your God that has ensured that you have come through the trials and tribulations you have come through, to bring you to this moment right now, hearing my words to you.

My beloved children, I stand at the door and knock, and if you open the door I will come in and we will sit down and have a meal together. I am the author and the finisher of your faith. I have called you by name. You are chosen and not forsaken. Before I created the heavens and the earth I planned for you to be receiving my words now. I am now lifting the veil. The scales are now falling from your eyes.

There is nothing to fear because my perfect love expels all fear. You aren't going into the unknown, you are coming into relationship with me, the Lord your God. You are so precious in my eyes. You are fearfully and wonderfully made in My image. You are My masterpiece, you and your family.

Come home, come running home. I am the Prince of Peace.

Even though your life hasn't been as challenging as other men and women walking the earth today, I know every moment of your life, when you have struggled and battled with thoughts in your mind. The battles that you have had have been hidden to the world, but I have seen every one of those battles. The times when you have felt condemned, guilty, shamed, fearful, frustrated, angry, bitter, resentful. I know each and every one of the experiences that you have had where you have been hurt. I have seen every tear that you have ever shed, and I have caught them in my bottle.

You have had your reasons for not turning to me but now I am calling you into my arms. I want to show you all the unfailing love I showed to David. I want to straighten out the crooked paths in your life.

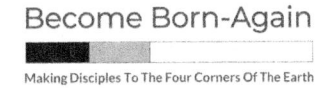

My way is perfect. I am the gate. I am the light of the world, and what I have chosen you to be living in and through is the most profound move that I have made upon the earth since I walked the earth.

My beloved, you and your parents and your grandparents and your great grandparents, you have been lied to and you have been deceived through your lives. My people walking the earth today have been lied to and deceived through their lives. I have allowed sin and the love of money, which is a root of all evil, I have allowed these things to pollute the earth. I have allowed evil to prosper.

I have seen everything. I have seen the corruption in my church. I have seen how corrupted the education system has become. I have seen every lie ever spoke by every single politician. I have seen every false and misleading headline from mainstream media. I have seen all the corruption, all the deception and all the evil within the pharmaceutical industry. I have seen the proliferation in the sexualization of women and also the sexualization of teenagers and children. I have watched and I have been disgusted because I detest a lying tongue. I detest a heart that plots evil. I detest feet that race to do wrong. I detest those who sow discord in the family. I detest those that murder the innocent. I detest haughty eyes.

I have allowed everything that has been taking place to take place, but now in 2022, my grace and my mercy upon the rulers, the controllers, the leaders, on those living in deep, dark sin, on those who truly have a love of money, which is a root of all evil, my grace and my mercy is truly coming to an end.

My beloved, what you are seeing in the world, what you are experiencing since 2020 is the proliferation of evil, the proliferation of darkness, the proliferation of lies, of deception, of corruption, the proliferation of planned evil, but I the Lord your God, I work in all things for good for those who love me and those who live according to my purpose for them, and my plans for you my beloved and your family, all your precious family that I have in the palm of my hand, my plans for you all are plans for good and not for disaster, to give you a future and a hope.

As you haven't yet received me the Lord your God as your Lord and Saviour, I know there have been many mixed feelings and emotions that you have battled with during the last two years. I know the decisions that you have made and the choices that you have made that had been based upon lies and deception, and so I know how you have had moments and periods battling with feelings of embarrassment, of shame, of guilt, of shock as you have sometimes began opening up to the reality of what has been taking place.

And I know also when you have had periods where in your mind you have felt like if you face into the truth of what has been taking place, that you will be condemned. But my beloved, there is no condemnation for those who belong to me, Christ Jesus.

My arms are wide open for you and your family. I meet you wherever you are. I have always loved you and I will always love you. Come home and Heaven will rejoice.

You are mine. You are chosen and not forsaken, and my perfect love expels all fear.

February 19th 2023

I Will Not Allow ANYONE To Take Away Your ANOINTING, Says The Lord

My beloved child, YOU are chosen by me.

YOU are anointed, and I the Lord your God will not allow anyone in your life currently, and anyone that will seek to come into your life or to speak into your life, to take away THE ANOINTING THAT IS UPON YOUR LIFE. This includes your brothers and your sisters, and this includes those who are at every single level of the established church system.

I am giving you wisdom and revelation now for you to have even greater DISCERNMENT by my Spirit, as you continue in your deepening PERSONAL RELATIONSHIP WITH ME the Lord your God.

The enemy FIRSTLY tried to kill you.

The enemy tried to kill what I was beginning to birth in you, before I had given you the revelation of me and who you are in me, the Lord your God.

Next, when the enemy realised that my hand is upon your life, and that the enemy could not kill you, the enemy began to bring LIES into your life.

LIES coming into your mind and LIES coming from the spoken and written words of people that have been in your life

Alongside the lies of the enemy, for the enemy is the father of lies, you began to receive FALSE ACCUSATIONS.

You began to receive SLANDEROUS comments.

You began to receive MOCKING comments.

You began to receive comments from people who are ENVIOUS of you.

You began to receive comments from people who are JEALOUS of you.

You began to experience comments, accusations and slurs from people who are PRIDEFUL.

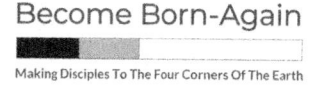

You have heard people trying to TWIST THE WORDS that you have spoken, the words that you have written.

You have had people QUESTIONING your relationship with me the Lord your God.

You have had people who have been in a relationship with me for longer than you, trying to BELITTLE THE THINGS YOU ARE DOING, for you have not been in a relationship with me as long as they have.

My beloved, fearfully and wonderfully made child, through every single trial and tribulation that you have experienced in your life, through everything that the enemy has thrown at you, including the times when you have felt surrounded on all sides by 10,000 enemies, I the Lord your God have been with you, for I AM FOR YOU AND NOT AGAINST YOU.

NO WEAPON THAT HAS EVER BEEN FORMED AGAINST YOU HAS EVER PROSPERED, and no weapon from this moment going forward will ever prosper, says I the Lord your God, AND EVERY TONGUE THAT RISES UP AGAINST YOU, YOU WILL CONDEMN, for that is a heritage of the servants of me, the Lord your God.

MY HAND IS MIGHTY UPON YOU.

There is an ANOINTING that I have placed upon your life that the kingdom of darkness has been so desperate to STEAL, to TAKE AWAY, to bring DOUBT, to bring CONFUSION.

My beloved child, alongside ALL THE OTHER ATTEMPTS OF THE ENEMY to pull you away from living your life worthy of the calling that you have received, the enemy too tries to bring DOUBT. To bring DOUBTS into your mind about what you are doing for me, as you are serving me, as you are being my hands and feet, as you are living your life as MY GLORY CARRIER.

The enemy has tried to get you to EXPLAIN YOURSELF, TO EXPLAIN WHAT YOU ARE DOING.

My beloved child, the reason that I have ordained for you to receive my words now, is that I the Lord your God say ENOUGH IS ENOUGH OF THE ENEMY TRYING TO QUENCH MY SPIRIT THAT IS AT WORK WITHIN YOU.

ENOUGH IS ENOUGH of any of your brothers and sisters being used as a vessel for the enemy, to try and bring doubt, to try and bring confusion, TO TRY AND SILENCE YOUR

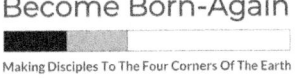

VOICE, FOR I THE LORD WILL NOT BE SILENCED, and I the Lord your God, the Lion of Judah, are BEGINNING TO ROAR IN YOUR LIFE, my beloved child.

With your faith in me the Lord your God and in me alone, with you NO LONGER IN ANY WAY LOOKING TO PLEASE MAN, and instead every single day looking to please me the Lord your God and me alone - when you take my Word, when you speak my Word, when you declare my Word, when you decree my Word - my promise to you, my beloved child, is that BLAZING COALS OF FIRE, TONGUES OF FIRE, are going to be SHOOTING OUT WORDS INTO THE KINGDOM OF DARKNESS.

POWERS AND PRINCIPALITIES OF DARKNESS are going to be OBLITERATED.

ANCESTRAL CURSES are going to be DESTROYED.

GENERATIONAL CURSES are going to be DESTROYED.

STRONGMEN are going to be BOUND UP AND THROWN INTO THE LAKE OF FIRE.

SOUL TIES are going to be DESTROYED.

Every single DEMON is going to be CAST OUT of other people that are coming into your life, in my name, for my glory, for I am the King of glory, and I have been given the NAME ABOVE ALL NAMES.

Oh my beloved child, I the Lord your God, I AM LOOSENING YOUR TONGUE.

THE FIRE, MY FIRE, THE FIRE OF MY SPIRIT, MY DEVOURING FIRE, is going to be on your tongue from this moment going forward.

I HAVE MADE YOU THE HEAD AND NOT THE TAIL.

I have given you ALL AUTHORITY to TRAMPLE upon lions and cobras, to CRUSH fierce lions and serpents UNDER YOUR FEET.

You RESIST the devil and he FLEES from you.

Thank you my beloved child for hearing my words, for receiving my words, and thank you my beloved child, for EVERYTHING that you have done for my kingdom and for EVERYTHING you are going to do from this moment going forward, not by your strength, not by your might, but and by my Spirit, for I have put my Spirit into you and greater is the Spirit that is in you than the spirit that is in the world.

My beloved child, it is not you that lives but I THE LORD THAT LIVES IN YOU.

Your eyes have not seen, your ears have not heard and your mind has not yet conceived what I the Lord your God have got planned for you because you love me.

My will be done, on earth as it is in heaven, in your life and in the lives of every man, woman and child walking the earth and that will walk the earth, says I the Sovereign Lord.

April 27th 2023

I Am Beginning To Open My People's Eyes To The SCALE, DEPTH & SIGNIFICANCE Of The Calling That Is Upon Their Life, Says The Lord

My beloved, look around at the nation's! Look and be amazed, for I am doing something in your own day, something you wouldn't even believe even if someone told you about it.

The ACCELERATION has begun!

The QUICKENING has begun!

The EXPANDING TERRITORY has begun!

The OUTPOURING OF MY SPIRIT has begun!

The TANGIBLE EXPERIENCES OF MY GLORY has begun!

The FULFILMENT OF MY PROMISES has begun!

The SUDDEN, PROFOUND CULMINATION OF DIFFERENT THINGS that have been going on, has begun!

The SUDDEN BREAKTHROUGHS have begun!

The MOVE OF MY SPIRIT has begun!

My beloved child, your eyes have not seen, your ears have not heard and your mind has not yet conceived what I the Lord your God have got planned for YOU because you love me.

Since early 2020 I began SENDING THE LOCUSTS INTO THE LIVES OF MY PEOPLE.

I began to PUT THEM IN THE REFINERS FIRE.

I began to allow the enemy to do EVERYTHING HE POSSIBLY COULD to destroy my people, but I have been with my people in the refiner's fire, just like Shadrach, Meshach and Abednego.

MY HAND IS MIGHTY UPON YOUR LIFE AND THE LIVES OF ALL MY PEOPLE ACROSS THE FLAT, STATIONARY EARTH THAT I CREATED.

Now it has been 3 YEARS IN THE REFINERS FIRE.

The PURIFICATION, the SANCTIFICATION and the CONSECRATION OF MY PEOPLE has been ALMOST UNBEARABLE for my people to endure, including you.

But my beloved child, my Word tells you in Romans 8 verse 28, I the Lord your God, I WORK IN ALL THINGS IN YOUR LIFE FOR GOOD because you love me, and because you live according to my purpose for you.

And now in 2023 and beyond, I am beginning to give my people DIVINE WISDOM AND REVELATION OF THE CALLING THAT IS UPON THEIR LIFE.

I am beginning to open my people's eyes to the SCALE, to the DEPTH, to the SIGNIFICANCE of the calling that is upon their life.

More and more and more of my people are beginning to live their life worthy of the calling that they have received, and that is TO BE MY GLORY CARRIER... TO BE MY HANDS AND FEET ACROSS THE EARTH.

My beloved, I the Lord was anointed with the Holy Spirit and with power.

YOU HAVE BEEN ANOINTED WITH THE HOLY SPIRIT AND WITH POWER.

YOU are going to go around doing good and healing all who are oppressed by the devil. The Spirit of the Sovereign Lord is upon you, for I the Lord has anointed YOU to bring good news to the poor.

I am sending YOU to comfort the broken-hearted and to proclaim that captives will be released and prisoners will be freed.

I am sending YOU to tell those who mourn that the time of I the Lord's favour has come, and with it the day of God's anger against their enemies.

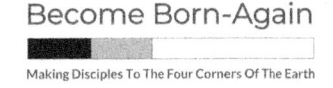

To all my people who mourn in Israel, I will give a crown of beauty for ashes, a joyous blessing instead of mourning, festive praise instead of despair. In their righteousness they will be like great oaks that I the Lord has planted for my own glory. They will rebuild the ancient ruins, repairing cities destroyed long ago. They will revive them, though they have been deserted for many generations.

Foreigners will be your servants. They will feed your flocks and plough your fields and tend your vineyards. YOU will be called priests of the Lord, ministers of our God. YOU will feed on the treasures of the nations and boast in their riches. Instead of shame and dishonour YOU will enjoy a double share of honour.

YOU will possess a double portion of prosperity in your land, and EVERLASTING JOY WILL BE YOURS. For I the Lord loves justice. I hate robbery and wrongdoing. I WILL faithfully reward my people for their suffering and make an everlasting covenant with them.

YOUR descendants will be recognised and honoured among the nations. Everyone will realise that they are a people that I the Lord has blessed.

YOU my beloved child are going to be overwhelmed with joy in me the Lord your God, for I have dressed you with the clothing of salvation and draped you in a robe of righteousness.

YOU are like a bridegroom dressed for his wedding or a bride with her jewels.

I the Sovereign Lord will show my justice to the nations of the world. Everyone will praise me. My righteousness will be like a garden in early spring, with plants springing up everywhere.

My beloved child, you have received the Holy Spirit and He lives within you, so you don't need anyone to teach you what is true, for the Spirit teaches you everything you need to know, and what He teaches is true. It is not a lie. So just as He has taught you, REMAIN IN FELLOWSHIP WITH ME THE LORD YOUR GOD.

I am giving YOU the power to perform unusual miracles. When handkerchiefs or aprons that have merely touched your skin are placed on sick people, they will be HEALED OF THEIR DISEASES AND EVIL SPIRITS WILL BE EXPELLED.

My beloved child, my Word tells you and all my chosen people in Psalms 105 verse 15, "Do NOT touch my chosen people and do NOT hurt my prophets".

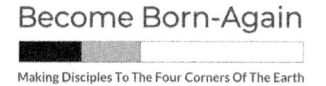

My beloved child you know that in my Word, there are four major prophets - Isaiah, Jeremiah, Ezekiel, and Daniel. As you are receiving my words now, YOU ARE RECEIVING A FRESH ANOINTING - the same anointing that was on the major prophets.

My beloved child, I AM RELEASING INTO YOUR LIFE THE ELIJAH ANOINTING, THE ELISHA ANOINTING, and my beloved child, I am going to be using YOU to RELEASE THE SAME ANOINTINGS that you have received into other people, and that THEY TOO will RELEASE THE SAME ANOINTINGS that they have received.

OH MY BELOVED CHILD, CAN YOU NOW BEGIN TO SEE WHAT I AM DOING ACROSS THE EARTH?

Hear this you leaders of the people. Listen, ALL who live in the land. In ALL your history, have you ever seen anything like this before? Tell your children about it in the years to come and tell your children to tell their children. PASS THE STORY DOWN FROM GENERATION TO GENERATION.

My beloved child, you know of my servants David, Noah, Moses, Joshua, Ruth, Samuel, Job, Mary.

You know of my prophets Hosea, Joel, Amos, Obadiah, Jonah, Micah, Nahum, Habakkuk, Zephaniah, Haggai, Zechariah, Malachi.

You know of my disciples in my Word, you know of the Apostles in my Word. Peter, Andrew, James, John, Simon, Paul, Matthew, Bartholomew, Philip, James, Thomas, Matthias, Nathaniel Mark, Zebedee, Simon, Timothy.

My beloved child, IT IS ONE SPIRIT. THE SAME SPIRIT THAT WAS IN ALL MY PROPHETS, ALL MY DISCIPLES, ALL MY APOSTLES, IT IS THE SAME SPIRIT THAT I HAVE PUT IN YOU, and greater is the Spirit that is in you than the spirit that is in the world.

YOU CAN DO AND YOU WILL DO ALL THINGS THROUGH ME, the Lord your God who gives you strength.

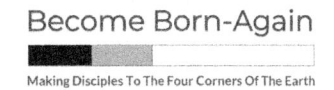

The same anointing that was on all my people is upon you, my beloved child, and your eyes have not seen, your ears have not heard and your mind has not yet conceived what I the Lord your God have got planned for you AND ALL MY PEOPLE across the flat, stationary Earth, because you love me, because you are my chosen people. YOU ARE MY HANDS AND FEET.

My beloved child, YOU will do the same things that I did and even greater things. YOU will be able to say to ANY MOUNTAIN may be lifted up and thrown into the sea, and because YOU HAVE MY FAITH, YES MY FAITH which I am releasing into your life right now, IT WILL HAPPEN.

Remember my Word in Matthew 21:22 - "You can pray for anything, and because you have faith you will receive it".

My beloved child, all this may seem impossible to you now, for you are a part of a small remnant of my people, but is it impossible for me? says I, the Lord of Heaven's Armies.

My Kingdom come, my will be done, in earth as it is in heaven, says I, the Sovereign Lord.

June 15th 2023

I Am Giving You The Key To Open The Door To Your Biggest Ever Breakthroughs, Says The Lord

My beloved child, you are receiving my message now, for I desire to give you and your brothers and sisters **absolute clarity as to what is the key that is going to open the door.**

You are wondering **"What door am I talking about?"**

I am talking about the door of **breakthrough**.

I am talking about the door of **healing**.

I am talking about the door of **deliverance**.

I am talking about the door of **long-term prayers being answered**.

I am talking about the door of **me fulfilling promises in my Word**.

I am talking about the door that brings **peace and joy every single day**.

I am talking about the door that is going to **set people free from bondage and from slavery**.

I am talking about the door that hundreds of millions of my followers have not yet walked through.

I am talking about the door that is **going to release my people**.

I am talking about the door that is going to **bring family reconciliation**.

I am talking about the door that is going to **bring financial blessings**.

I am talking about the door that is going to **free people from mental health oppression**.

I am talking about **the door that so few of my people have been willing to walk through** so far in their relationship with me, the Lord your God.

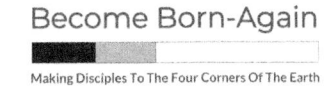

I am talking about what most of my people see as a GIANT door.

Most people **see this door as IMPENETRABLE**.

Most people see this door as **a door that is not for them to walk through**.

Most people **have a fear of this door**.

Most people **have dismissed this door**.

Most people **look the other way for an alternative door for their breakthrough to come**.

Most people are so desperate for me to bring changes in their life, **but they keep turning away from this door that is in front of them**.

The door, that once you and my people step through you will begin to experience my glory, a fulfilment of my promises from my Word, you will begin to experience breakthrough, healings, reconciliation, blessing upon blessing upon blessing…

THE DOOR IS GOING TELLING COMPLETE STRANGERS THAT I LOVE THEM.

In your conversations where you are speaking to complete strangers about how I saved your life, **you will also be saying to them "Can I pray for you?"**

THE KEY TO OPEN THIS DOOR, is for you to be truly willing to DENY YOURSELF, to pick up your cross DAILY and follow me.

You will take this key and use this key to open this door, not by your strength, not by your might, **but by my Spirit.**

My beloved child, SHARE my message here with your brothers and sisters.

If you could only **begin to comprehend the hundreds of millions of my people,** of my followers, **who need to take hold of this key** to open what has been this impenetrable, huge door, you would be **shouting this message from the rooftops**.

My people have been **living self-centredly**.

My people have been **focused on their own prayer requests**.

My people have **not been freely giving, just as they have freely received**.

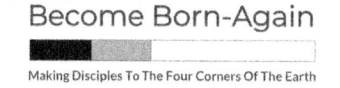

My people have been living with a fear of man, but I have not given them a spirit of fear, but of power, of love and of a sound mind.

My people have been in sin, because it is a sin to know what you ought to do and then not do it.

My people have been **living with timidity**.

My people have been **keeping their faith to themselves**.

My people have been **focused on themselves, on their own circumstances, on their own family, on their own finances, on their own prayer requests**, and they have **not been going out answering the prayers of other people** by being my hands and feet, to tell the **lost**, to tell the **broken**, to tell those in **slavery**, to tell those living with **brokenness**, to tell those with **stony hearts**, to tell those living with **unforgiveness**, THAT I LOVE THEM.

My beloved child, I have chosen **you** to be one of my disciples.

I have chosen **you** to be one of my glory carriers.

I have chosen **you** to be my hands and feet.

Once you truly step through this door, filled with my Spirit, because you have humbled yourself, you have denied yourself, you have surrendered your entire life to me and it is not your will that you are desiring to follow but it is my will, **YOU WILL NEVER TURN BACK**.

Once you go through this door, you will see a manifestation of my glory in ways in which you have never seen before.

You will receive blessing upon blessing upon blessing.

You will see me move mightily in your life.

You will see me move in the lives of your loved ones in ways in which you have never experienced before.

You will live in joy and peace.

The fruit of the Spirit will be what you are exhibiting each and every day.

You will experience total and complete freedom.

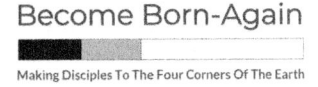

You will no longer be in slavery, no longer be in bondage.

You will no longer be burdened for as you cast your burdens upon me, because I care for you, **you will be set free as one of my glory carriers**.

ALL MY PROMISES TO YOU IN MY WORD, from the beginning of Genesis to the end of Revelation, **are yes and amen IN MY PERFECT TIME.**

Now **GO** when I ask you to go.

SPEAK when I ask you to speak.

STAY SILENT when I ask you to stay silent.

PROPHESY when I ask you to prophesy.

LAY HANDS ON PEOPLE when I ask you to lay hands on people.

OFFER TO PRAY FOR PEOPLE when I ask you to pray for people.

FREELY GIVE as you have freely received.

Live your life worthy of the calling with which you have received from me the Lord of lords, the King of kings, the Alpha and the Omega, the beginning and the end.

I AM the author and the finisher of your faith, and my kingdom come, my will be done, on earth as it is in heaven.

January 19th 2022

I Am Raising Up An Army That Are BREAKING EVERY CHAIN, Says The Lord

I am truly giving you the eyes to see and the ears to hear with what I am doing in the world. I have removed the scales from your eyes. You will never again be deceived by man. You will never again be deceived by false prophets, false teachers, because I the Lord your God have poured out My Spirit in you and, through, a profound increase in the wisdom that I am giving you right now, you will have discernment like you have never had before. So that when you hear a message from a teacher, a preacher, a prophet, my spirit upon you and within you will convict you to know when you are watching and listening to a false prophet or when you are hearing a message that comes from me. A message of truth, a message of hope.

I have called you by name. My hand is mighty upon you. I have anointed your head with oil, you and your family. I have chosen you to walk by faith, not by sight. I am birthing in you a David and you are going to be taking the head off Goliath. I have given you all the power and all the authority in the spiritual realm to trample upon lions and cobras and to crush fears lions and serpents under your feet. I have put my spirit within you and greater is a spirit that is in you than the spirit that is in the world. I have made a table for you in the presence of your enemies, but you have no fear. My perfect love expels all fear. I have not given you a spirit of fear but of power, of Love and of a sound mind. The weapons that you fight with are not of the world. On the contrary, they have divine power to break down strongholds and I have given you all power and all authority to destroy strongmen, to destroy demonic powers and principalities, in your life and in the lives of other people that I will be bringing into your life.

The enemy is under your feet. Death is defeated. I the Lord your God defeated death and the power of sin through my life. Through My crucifixion. Through my death, through my burial and through my resurrection by the power of the Holy Spirit. I am the resurrection and the life. I am the King of glory. I am the name of ALL names. I am the Lord of lords and King of Kings and I am roaring. I am roaring in your life. I am roaring in the lives of millions and millions of people and I the Lord your God am only just getting started. I am only just getting started.

I am reaching the end of my patience with the sinners, with those who have been plotting evil, with those speaking lying words from their tongues. I see everything. I know everything. I have seen every single conversation, every single plan that has ever been made, that has brought destruction upon my people. I have seen every single meeting done in dark, in secret. I know all hearts and minds, and my heart weeps. My heart weeps for all those currently living in sin and darkness, deceived. Yes, My people have been deceived, you and all people have been deceived, throughout their entire lives and yes, I the Lord your God have allowed this because I have been bringing my people, I've been bringing the earth to this moment in time. 2020, 2021, 2022. This is MY plan. This is MY agenda. I laugh at the wicked, I scoff at their plans. Every knee shall bow in my name. People have been planning all kinds of things but MY will is going to be done, and my well is being done. I the Lord your God, the King of kings and Lord of lords. The Alpha and the Omega, the resurrection and the life, the good shepherd, the light of the world. Yes, I am the light of the world and I am shining light into all the darkness.

Everything done is done in the dark is being been brought into the light for My glory. For I am the Lord of Heavens armies and I am roaring. I am rising up my army and every chain will break in my name by my blood. You My people are fearfully and wonderfully made. Have no fear. I have called you by name. I have given you ALL the authority in the spiritual realm. You and my beloved precious warriors, the mighty mighty men and women of God who already know that their identities in me and the millions and millions of people walking the earth today who I have put the truth of the world in them. But they haven't yet surrendered their life to me. But it is coming because I am the one who lifts the veil. I am the one who removes the scales from people's eyes. This is my plan. This is my agenda for My glory in my perfect time.

YOU are going to be ROARING in your prayer life, for I the Lord your God, the Lord of Heavens armies has spoken. YOU are going to be praying in the valley of dry bones and you are going to be seeing the dry bones come alive as you speak prophetic words into the dry bones of your life, of your family, of your loved ones, of your friends, of your circumstances and of people's lives whom you don't yet know. Yes, I am going to be bringing people into your life and you will be speaking into their life. You will be prophesying into their life. You will be breathing life into them through My words, for the glory of your Father in heaven. And through all of this, you will be giving all the glory, all the praise and all the honour to your Father in heaven, for I the Lord your God has spoken.

My hand is MIGHTY upon you. I have anointed your head with oil. I have taught put angels in place around you and upon your family and through your faith, through your pure faith in me, and through your trust a My timing, through your patience, through your prayers, through your worshipping in spirit and in truth, you are going to see breakthroughs in your life for I the Lord your God have spoken. Breakthrough is coming. Resurrection of lost loved ones is coming. Restoration of broken family relationships is coming. Healing is coming. The mentally oppressed are being healed in my name by my spirit, for I the Lord of Heavens army has spoken. I am the miracle worker. I am your healer. I am the world's healer. By the strides on my back, my people are healed. By my people's faith in me they will be healed. I am healing now physical afflictions. I am healing mental afflictions. I am breaking iron chains of bondage in my name by my blood, for the glory of the Father, your Abba Father, the Creator of the heavens and the earth.

And now, I bring you peace. I the Lord your God speak to you now and say peace, be still. Peace, be still. The peace I give you is a gift the world cannot give you. I have not given you a spirit of fear, but of power, of love and have a sound mind. I have given you ALL power in the spiritual realm. All power. My beloved I have given you ALL power. Let me say that again, I have given you ALL power in the spiritual realm, and through my spirit been upon you the FIRE of the Holy Ghost working through you and coming from your tongue, through your words of prayer of intercession, taking my word, YOU are going to be seeing me move in your life and in the lives of other people that you pray for like never before. You are going to be led into floods of tears as I the Lord your God move in your life and I will leave you in awe and wonder. I will leave you open mouthed, your eyes will be wide open you will be crying tears of joy. Tears of for breakthrough, for resurrection, for provision, for finances, for blessings, for love for joy for peace, for addictions been broken, for healing taking place. Miracles signs and wonders I am bringing it into your life for I the Lord your God have spoken. And through all of what is coming into your life, you will be in peace, filled with my joy, smiling radiantly at people that see you carrying my glory, because I have called you to be my glory carrier. Yes, you have been called by me, the Lord your God, to be my glory carrier.

Your eyes haven't seen, your ears haven't heard and your minds haven't conceived, what I the Lord your God have prepared for you who love me.

Peace, be still. Peace, be still.

January 26th 2023

I Am Loosening Your Tongue, Says The Lord

My beloved, before I created the heavens and the earth, I ordained for you to receive my message to you now.

As you receive my words to you now, I the Lord your God, the King of kings, the Lord of lords, the author and the finisher of your faith, I AM LOOSENING YOUR TONGUE.

From this moment going forward, by my Spirit, you will be SPEAKING MY NAME AND SPEAKING MY WORD OUT LOUD MORE THAN YOU EVER HAVE DONE.

I am setting a FIRE deep down inside of you NOW.

THE SHACKLES ARE DESTROYED NOW.

NO MORE WILL THE SPIRIT OF TIMIDITY HOLD YOU BACK from speaking my name boldly, from speaking my Word boldly.

NO MORE will you stay silent whilst negative thoughts, feelings and emotions overwhelm you.

NO MORE will you be like a rabbit in the headlights when trials and tribulations come into your life.

My beloved child, my fearfully and wonderfully made child, as I loosen your tongue now, as my devouring fire falls upon you, you are going to find there is a power, there is an authority, there is an anointing on your life, to speak my name BOLDLY, to declare my Word BOLDLY. To not just walk by faith and not by sight, but to TALK BY FAITH NOT BY SIGHT.

ALL MY PROMISES TO YOU ARE YES AND AMEN, IN MY PERFECT TIME.

The light is going to penetrate the darkness in your life and in the lives of people around you, unlike you've ever seen before.

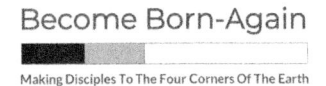

As you speak my name, as you confess my name, as you declare my name, as you decree my name, as you take hold of my Word, as you speak my Word over your life, over your circumstances, over your family, over people you have never met before, my beloved child, there will now start to be blazing coals of fire coming from your tongue. Yes, coming from your tongue.

NO MORE, my beloved child, will you live in your comfort zone.

From this moment going forward, you are going to BEGIN LIVING OUTSIDE OF YOUR COMFORT ZONE EVERY DAY.

NO MORE timidity.

NO MORE apprehension.

NO MORE worry.

NO MORE concern.

NO MORE fear.

NO MORE comparing yourself to others.

NO MORE heaviness.

NO MORE confusion.

NO MORE self-pity.

NO MORE self-condemnation.

NO MORE of your old self.

NO MORE compromise.

NO MORE OF YOURSELF.

My beloved child, it is not you that live, but I the Lord your God that lives in you.

My will be done, on earth as it is in heaven.

July 6th 2022

If You Want To Enjoy Life & See Many Happy Days, Keep Your Tongue From Speaking Evil & Your Lips From Telling Lies

My beloved, among all the parts of your body, your tongue is a flame of fire when you allow it. Your tongue is a whole world of wickedness, corrupting your entire body. It can set your whole life on fire, for it is set on fire by hell itself.

My beloved, this is the same for every single man, woman and child walking the earth, every single one of your family members, your brothers, your sisters, people in your life whom I haven't yet lifted the veil.

My beloved, you will be experiencing cursing, lies and threats coming from the tongues of others. You will have been shocked at the behaviour of people in your own home, your brothers, your sisters, and people who don't even know you. But remember my beloved that their own tongue will ruin them and all who see them will shake their heads in scorn.

When I send my Word out, it does not return to me void, it accomplishes all that I desire and it prospers everywhere that I send it. I know all hearts. I have seen every single lie that you have ever spoken, that everyone in your life has ever spoken.

You have experienced the wickedness of the tongue firsthand in your life. My beloved, prepare yourself for more shocking behaviour of people attempting to speak into your life. My beloved, keep your eyes focused on me, the author and the finisher of your faith. I am for you and not against you.

Rejoice when trials come your way. Rejoice when battles come, because you know that the testing of your faith produces perseverance and through everything that I have ever allowed in your life, and through everything that I will allow to come into your life, I am continually refining you by fire. I am purifying you. I am sanctifying you. I am cleansing you. I am completely separating you from the world. Remember, my beloved, you are in the world but not of the world. Greater is the Spirit that is in you than the spirit that is in the world.

I will hide you in the shelter of my presence, safe from those who conspire against you. I shelter you in my presence far from accusing tongues.

My Beloved, if you want to enjoy life and see many happy days, keep your tongue from speaking evil and your lips from telling lies.

The crooked heart will not prosper. The lying tongue tumbles into trouble.

Keep surrendering everything in your life to me. Seek my Kingdom and my righteousness first, and all else will be given unto you, says I, the Lord of Heaven's Armies.

June 21st 2022

Speak Life Not Death, Love Not Fear, Says The Lord

My beloved, there is power in your tongue to speak life, or to speak death. There is power in your actions to share love or to share fear.

My beloved, I am calling you to SPEAK LIFE into your life, into your entire family's life, into the lives of your brothers and your sisters, and I am calling you to speak life into the lives of unbelievers. When you speak about acts of evil, when you share information about acts of evil, you are spreading fear.

My beloved, the only fear that you should be speaking about, is the reverent fear of me, the Lord your God.

I haven't given you or your brothers and sisters a spirit of fear, but of power, of love and of a sound mind.

I am calling you my beloved, to fix your eyes on the things above, not the things below. I am calling you to SATURATE YOUR LIFE EACH DAY with the things of my Kingdom, reading my Word, hearing my Word, speaking my Word, worshipping me in spirit and in truth, saturating your entire being with the things of my Kingdom, because remember my beloved, you are in the world but you are not of the world, I have called you out of the darkness and into my glorious light.

Remember my beloved, there is power on your tongue and there is power from your actions. Your tongue can speak life or death and your actions can spread love or spread fear.

My beloved, SPEAK LIFE. Let your actions share my love, share my agape love.

May your actions shine light into the darkness of those who I haven't yet brought into salvation. My beloved, I have called you by name from your mother's womb, to be my glory carrier.

Thank you for hearing my voice.

Thank you for receiving my words.

Thank you for following my will for your life.

My beloved, the more that you saturate your life each day with the things of my Kingdom, the more that I will be saturating you with my glory.

Prepare for more and more tears as you experience more and more of my goodness, of my joy, of my love, of my peace.

My Peace is a gift to you that the world cannot give you, and my peace surpasses all understanding.

My beloved, you are my masterpiece, says I, the Lord of Heaven Armies.

January 18th 2022

STOP Fear Mongering, Speak Life NOT Death Into The World, Says The Lord

My beloved, there are many, many false teachers and false prophets walking the earth right now. There are many false teachers and false prophets, speaking doom, gloom and apocalypse into people's lives, but I am the light of the world. You are my hands and feet. I have called you by name. I have given you all the power and all the authority in a spiritual realm to prophesy into the dry bones, for the dead to come alive.

There are prophets out there speaking doom, gloom and death into people's lives, but I say NO!!! I am the way, the true and the life, and you are my chosen people. I am raising the dead to life, and I have had enough of the false teachers, the false prophets, speaking apocalypse.

When have I said this is the apocalypse?

The enemy has deceived all the nations, even the elect her being deceived. I am doing a new thing for my glory. I am exposing all the works of evil, of darkness that I have seen through all the generations. Everything done in dark is being brought to light, for I the Lord of Heaven Armies have spoken. I laugh at the plans of the wicked. I scoff at the rulers. I am going to destroy the powers and principalities of evil of darkness. Every knee shall bow.

You, my beloved, my fearfully and wonderfully made army, greater is the spirit in you that the spirit that is in the world. You can pray for anything, and because you have the faith that I have given you, you will receive it.

You, my beloved, have been called to walk in the whole truth. I have called you by name. I have put my spirit in you. My spirit guides you into all truth, and you are never again going to speak doom, gloom, apocalypse, darkness, death into anyone life. You are going to speak life into people's lives. You are going to speak love into people's lives. The dry bones are going to come alive.

I, the Lord of Heaven Army, are doing a new thing. Everything that can be shaken, is being shaken. I am shaking the wicked and the evil, but you do not see it, because it comes from within. People may plan all kinds of things. People have been planning all kinds of things. People have been perpetrating evil because of their sinful nature, because of their love of money, which is the root of all evil. And I have seen everything and my heart has been weeping, weeping for the children, the devastation, the evil acts. The murderers and the deceivers. The families, the elderly.

But this is MY agenda. These are MY plans. Everything that has been happening, I have allowed to happen because before the creation of the heavens and the earth, I planned for 2020, 2021, 2022 to awaken my people, my beloved lost sheep, to awaken them to the truth of evil and to the truth of their sin nature.

And for my glory, I am awakening the masses. For My glory, I am giving people in positions of power and authority that have abused their power and the authority that I have given them, I am giving them nightmares. Yes nightmares. Yes I am showing them hell. I am showing that they are heading to hell. That they are on the wide path of sin that leads to death. I am convicting them in their hearts of what they have perpetrated, the evil that they have perpetrated.

Even when you don't see it, I am working. Even when you don't feel it, I am working. My divine justice is coming into the world. For my glory, yes, for I the Lord your God. I am the King of kings. I am the Lord of lords. I am the name above all names.

My light is shining more and more and more into the world into the hearts and minds of millions, and what will become billions of people. My people, my beloved, my precious lost sheep. This is My plan. This is My agenda for My glory. I am the King of glory. I am the Way, the Truth and the Life and no one comes to the Father except through me.

My beloved... the teachers, the preachers, the prophets that are speaking death, devastation, apocalypse, end of end days... they have been deceived. They are striking fear into My people, they are striking fear into the hearts of the unbelievers.

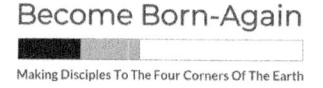

I have called you to speak truth, life, love, revival, awakening, glory into the lives of people in your life and the people I will be bringing into your life. The spiritually dead are going to be coming alive like never seen before. My presence is already on earth. It is I that lives in you. You are my hands and feet. Greater is the spirit in you than the Spirit that is in the world. You can do all things through me who gives you strength. The weapons that you fight with are not of the world. On the contrary, they have divine power to break down struggles. My presence, the Lord of Heaven's Armies is already upon the earth and my presence is coming into the earth, onto the world more and more and more, and I look down from heaven and I see everything. I see the wicked, the rulers, the false teachers. I see how Satan even masquerades as an angel of light.

This is ALL for MY glory. This is all what I have allowed to happen because now the world is seeing that the love of money is the root of all evil. People in high places have been bought, have been corrupted. My church has been infested with sin, with Freemasons, with Jesuits, but I see all hearts and minds. I have everyone in the palm of my hand. Yes, everyone walking the earth. NOTHING is going to stop what I am doing across the earth in 2022. NOTHING!

I have chosen you. You are my true remnant, purified by my blood, purified by my Holy Spirit, completely surrendered to me. My hand is mighty upon you. I have anointed your head with oil. I have appointed you, before the creation of the heavens and the earth, to be a prophet to the nations. I have only just begun working in your life. And you my beloved will never again be deceived by man. You will never again be deceived by false prophets, by false teachers, by false evangelists. I am now pouring out my spirit within you, upon you, through you. I am filling you now with my spirit, and my spirit guides you, my beloved, into ALL truth, and through my spirit guiding you, you will be devouring my word like NEVER before. You will be worshipping in spirit and in truth like never before.

You are going to be calling on my word in Jeremiah 33 verse three. Call on Me and I will answer. I will tell you things that haven't been shared, secret things that you do not know call on me and I will answer for I the Lord of Heaven's armies have spoken.

Peter replied, "Each of you must repent of your sins and turn to God, and be baptized in the name of Jesus Christ for the forgiveness of your sins. Then you will receive the gift of the Holy Spirit.

Acts 2:38

November 29th 2022

I Am Taking You From The Globe Deception To A Firmament Of Fire, Says The Lord

My beloved child, I have called you by name from your mother's womb, not just to have faith, not just to believe in me, not just to pray, not just to read my Word, not just to worship me - I have called you by name to be my disciple, to be my hands and feet, to be my glory carrier.

I the Lord your God am a devouring fire and my devouring fire is absolutely obliterating the globe deception.

One by one, as I destroy the deception through indoctrination of the globe earth, my chosen people are then ready for me to put A FIRMAMENT OF FIRE AROUND THEM.

YES, as my Word tells you, I created a firmament above the Earth, separating the waters above the firmament from the waters below the firmament.

YES, as my Word tells you, within this firmament I created lights to separate the day from the night. These lights shine down on the earth. I made two great lights, the greater one, the sun, to govern the day, and the lesser one, the moon, to govern the night. I also made the stars.

My beloved, fearfully and wonderfully made servant, I am calling you now to share the truth in my Word every day. No longer be afraid of speaking about the truth that the earth that you live on, that I created, is fixed, immovable, as my Word tells you.

So many of my people who are in relationship with me, still have not yet accepted that they have been deceived by man into thinking that they live on a globe spinning and flying through space, but remember, I am a devouring fire, and as you speak my Word, as you declare my Word, as you share my Word about my creation, the strongholds of deception in other people are going to be destroyed, and I will put a firmament of fire around you, so that no weapons formed against you will prosper, and every tongue that rises up against you, you will condemn, for that is a heritage of the servants of me, the Lord your God.

July 24th 2023

I Am Destroying The Deception Of Gravity, Says The Lord

My beloved child, I have chosen you to receive my message now about the term "**gravity**".

Throughout the whole of my Word, from the beginning of Genesis to the end of Revelation, **there is not one mention of the word "gravity".**

Over many, many years, I have allowed man to teach my people across the earth about **an unseen force that supposedly is the force which keeps everything and everyone that I created upon the earth miraculously held down, to what you have been told and taught is a globe shaped earth that is continuously spinning and is continually flying through space.**

My beloved child, **I make the wisdom of this world look foolish.**

Yes, there is **an unseen, miraculous force that is at work upon the earth**.

It is a force with **unimaginable power.**

It is a force that **defies human logic and reasoning.**

It is an unseen force **that is unstoppable.**

It is an unseen force that has a profound, life-changing impact on every man, woman, teenager, child and baby that is upon the earth today, that has ever been upon the earth and that will come into the world after I have created them and knitted them together in the depths of their mother's womb.

In ALL the scientific books, journals and papers, in the textbooks used within the **education system,** on the website **space.com**, on the **NASA** website, in the **New Scientist** magazines, this **incomprehensible** power, this **invisible** power, this **unstoppable** power, **this life-changing power that is present upon the earth, IS NOT MENTIONED.**

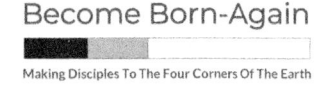

Become Born-Again

Making Disciples To The Four Corners Of The Earth

This incomprehensible, inconceivable, invisible, life-changing, life-giving, life-sustaining power IS MY SPIRIT.

I the Lord your God, **I am coming in power by my Spirit** into the lives of more and more men, women and children.

My unimaginable power is at work in the lives of more and more people.

THIS POWER RAISED ME FROM THE DEAD ON THE THIRD DAY, for I AM the resurrection and the life.

My beloved child, **FORGET MANMADE GRAVITY.**

Speak only about the power of my Spirit at work.

I the Lord your God are **destroying the deception of gravity,** as I am destroying **the deception of the Big Bang,** as I am destroying **the deception of the universe,** as I am destroying **the deception of the globe earth,** as I am **destroying the deception of evolution,** as I the Lord your God are **destroying EVERY SINGLE MANMADE DECEPTION that I have allowed.**

The **power of my Spirit** is coming upon more and more people.

More and more people are walking in power, in victory, in authority, and I have only just begun.

Talk only about the power of my Spirit.

NO LONGER HOLD BACK from telling people that they do not live on a spinning globe earth held down by gravity. Tell them that the earth that I created is fixed, immovable, and it will not be moved, and **the only invisible power that they should be desiring is the power of my Spirit, my Holy Spirit.**

My Kingdom come, my will be done, on earth as it is in heaven, says I, the King of kings, the Lord of lords, the Alpha and the Omega, the beginning and the end, the first and the last, the Holy One of Israel, the resurrection and the life.

I AM the Way, the Truth and the Life, and no-one can come to the Father except through me.

July 8th 2023

The Sound of Freedom Has Only Just Begun, And My Imminent Return Is Now Here, Says The Lord

My beloved child, you are receiving my message now for I desire to give you **wisdom and revelation regarding my film Sound of Freedom and my imminent return.**

Before I created the heavens and the earth, I planned out the lives of everyone that is apart of my film, Sound of Freedom.

Every single day of their life is written in my book.

Every single moment was laid out before a single day had passed.

Every single one of their ancestors, every single man and woman and child walking the earth, and everyone that has ever walked the earth, every day of their life is written in my book.

At the beginning of the year 2020, **I began to once again shake the heavens and the earth.** I began to **shine my light upon the gross darkness** that had covered the earth for hundreds and hundreds and hundreds of years.

My film Sound of Freedom is going to be seen by the eyes of hundreds of millions of my people walking the earth today.

This film is one of the intrinsic parts of my divine plan to bring in a new age.

My beloved child, you will have heard many voices speaking about **my imminent return.**

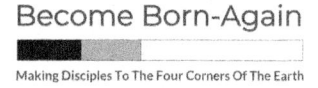

Every second of every day, I am coming down from heaven, mounted on a mighty angelic being, **to rescue my people** that have been in slavery and in bondage. One by one, I go down into the deep waters to rescue my chosen people from all their enemies - men, women and children - and every single time I give one of my people that I created the eyes to see and ears to hear, every single time I lift the veil, every single time the scales fall from their eyes, I fill them with my Spirit so that it is not they that live but I that live in them.

Yes, my beloved child, my imminent return to the lost, to the broken, to the helpless, to the hopeless, to those in slavery, to those in Egypt, to those with addictions, to those living with unforgiveness, to those living in poverty, my imminent return is truly imminent.

Sound the alarm in Jerusalem. Blow the ram's horn!

There is the sound of freedom in the spirit realm, and my people, men, women and children who I have already set free, who have a pure heart and clean hands, **they are doing greater and greater things to destroy the works of darkness.**

Powers and principalities of darkness are being destroyed by the prayers and the worship of my people.

More and more and more men, women and children are worshipping me in spirit and in truth.

More and more and more men, women and children **are standing in and are using the authority that I have given them,** to trample upon lions and cobras, to crush fierce lions and serpents under their feet.

All my chosen people are seated alongside me in heavenly places. They are lords. They are kings, and I AM the Lord of lords, I AM the King of kings.

I have only just begun bringing my people back from Egypt.

I have only just begun bringing my chosen people back from the north and the south and from the east and from the west.

I have only just begun giving gifts of my Spirit to my people.

My beloved child, **look around at the nation's! Look and be amazed,** for I am doing something in your own day, something that you wouldn't even believe even if someone told you about it.

Hear this you leaders of the people! Listen all who live in the land. **In all your history, have you ever seen anything like this before?** Tell your children about it in the years to come, and tell your children to tell their children. **Pass the story down of I the Lord your God beginning to bring in a new age from the year 2020, from generation to generation.**

You don't understand what I am doing now, but someday you will.

My beloved child, never ever again doubt my Sovereignty.

Never again doubt that people who plan and do wicked and evil things will be judged by me. They will not get away with it. I know all things I see all things.

My beloved child, also know that **I have every single child, of every single age,** no matter where they are across the earth today, in the palm of my hand. **They are mine.**

No matter what circumstances children are living in, no matter what children have been subjected to, no matter what evil children have experienced, they are MY precious children, and I will NEVER leave them nor forsake them.

My beloved child, across the entire earth, no eye has seen, no ear has heard and no mind has conceived what I the Lord have got planned for those who love me.

I have heard every single one of your prayers. For all the people that you have ever prayed for, remember, I surrendered my life on the cross to save their life. **I love them more than you can possibly comprehend.**

My beloved child, share this message with your brothers and sisters.

The sound of freedom has only just begun, and my imminent return upon the earth is now here, says I the Sovereign Lord.

January 18th 2023

I Could Have Explicitly Stated That The Earth Is Flat, Says The Lord

My beloved, you are receiving my message to you now, for I the Lord your God desire to give you wisdom and revelation about my creation.

Throughout my Word, starting from Genesis chapter one verse one, I describe my creation.

I describe the earth.

I describe the heavens.

I describe the sun.

I describe the moon.

I describe the stars.

In my Word I could have explicitly stated the shape of the earth that I created.

I could have explicitly stated that the earth is flat.

By me not stating explicitly that the earth that I created is flat, I the Lord your God, the King of kings, the Lord of lords, the Alpha and the Omega, the beginning and the end, the first and the last, I then allowed for the DECEPTION of the Big Bang.

The DECEPTION of the universe.

The DECEPTION of the solar system.

The DECEPTION of the planets.

The DECEPTION of the size of the sun.

The DECEPTION of the distance the sun is away from earth.

The DECEPTION of men walking on the moon.

The DECEPTION of evolution.

The DECEPTION of the globe earth spinning and flying through man made space.

My beloved child, can you now see how ALL OF THOSE DECEPTIONS ARE CONNECTED TOGETHER? Yes, including the DECEPTION OF GRAVITY. For without gravity, the entire globe earth deception collapses, and I the Lord your God, I am a jealous God, and I HAVE NOW SEEN ENOUGH OF MY PEOPLE BEING DECEIVED BY MAN.

I am truly lifting the veil on every deception that my people have been subjected to, that I have allowed.

I AM DESTROYING EVERY DECEPTION, says I the Lord your God.

THE VEIL IS TRULY BEING LIFTED.

I AM SETTING THE CAPTIVES FREE.

EVERY SINGLE MAN-MADE DECEPTION THAT HAS BEEN PUSHED AND PUSHED THROUGH A LIFETIME OF INDOCTRINATION IS BEING DESTROYED BY MY DEVOURING FIRE, says I the Lord of lords, the King of kings, the one true living God.

My beloved child, my Word tells you that unless you become like a little child, you will not see the kingdom of Heaven. My desire for you now, my call to you now, is for you to humble yourself, for you to be willing to forget every single thing that sinful, deceitful man has told you during your life, and yes, that includes people behind the pulpit.

My Spirit is your teacher.

My Spirit is the spirit of truth, and MY SPIRIT WILL LEAD YOU IN TO ALL TRUTH, AND MY WORD IS THE TRUTH.

I am the Lord of lords, the King of kings. I am the way, the truth and the life and no one comes to the Father except through me.

BY MY SWORD, I am DESTROYING the LEVIATHAN SPIRIT.

BY MY SWORD, I am DESTROYING the JEZEBEL SPIRIT

BY MY SWORD, I am DESTROYING the ANTICHRIST spirit, says I the Sovereign Lord.

Thank you, my beloved child, for humbling yourself and receiving wisdom and revelation from me, through my chosen servant Paul, who like you, I have called to be one of my glory carriers, to be my hands and feet.

My beloved child, I have put my Spirit into you, and the spirit that is in you is greater than the spirit that is in the world.

Trust me and me alone.

MY SPIRIT IS YOUR TEACHER, AND MY SPIRIT WILL LEAD YOU FOR THE REST OF YOUR LIFE INTO ALL TRUTH, says I the Sovereign Lord.

September 8th 2022

The Globe Earth Is An Idol, The Universe Is An Idol, Says The Lord

My beloved, the greatest deception that I have allowed my people across the earth to be indoctrinated by, is the globe earth.

It is the Leviathan spirit at work in the hearts of people across the entire earth that is currently stopping my chosen people from accepting that they have been deceived by man.

Pastors, preachers, evangelists, prophets are currently afraid of speaking out to share my Word, which is alive and powerful and sharper than the sharpest of two-edged swords, my Word that tells my people that the earth is fixed, immovable and will not be moved.

They don't want to cause disharmony. They don't want to cause friction. They don't want to cause division, but remember, I didn't come to bring peace to the earth, I came not to bring peace, but a sword.

Who may climb my mountain? Who may stand in my holy place? Only those whose hands and hearts are pure, who do not worship idols and never tell lies.

The globe earth is an idol.

The universe is an idol.

Don't let anyone capture you with empty philosophies and high-sounding nonsense that come from human thinking and from the spiritual powers of the world, rather than from me, the Lord your God.

My Word is alive and powerful. It is sharper than the sharpish two-edged sword, cutting between soul and spirit between joint and marrow. My Word exposes the innermost thoughts and desires of my people, both those who I have set free and those who I haven't yet set free.

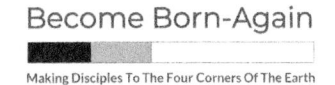

It is only I the Lord your God that can obliterate the Leviathan spirit. One by one I am obliterating the Leviathan spirit that has had a hold of my people. I am setting my people free from the deception of the globe earth.

I am beginning to move relentlessly in the lives of my chosen people. I am calling my people to forget everything that man has taught them, everything corrupted, deceived, sinful man has taught them, and to stand completely and absolutely on my Word, and to TRUST ME AND ME ALONE.

I am THE WAY, THE TRUTH AND THE LIFE, and no-one can come to the Father except through me.

My beloved, continue to speak the truth in love, growing in every way more and more like me, the Lord your God, because I am the head of my body, which is the church.

I am the King of glory, and I have called you by name from your mother's womb to be my glory carrier, says I, the Sovereign Lord.

March 9th 2023

My Word Reveals To You That The Earth That I Created Is FLAT, Says The Lord

My beloved, my Word tells you that I DETEST the PROUD.

My Word tells you that unless you become like a little child, you will not see my Kingdom.

I the Lord your God have allowed you and all my people upon the earth, GOING BACK TWO GENERATIONS, to be deceived through a lifetime of INDOCTRINATION, that the earth that I created is shaped as a GLOBE, that this GLOBE is spinning on its axis, that this GLOBE is flying at vast speeds through space, circling the sun, and that the "SOLAR SYSTEM" is also fly flying through what has been described by man as the "UNIVERSE" at speeds in which you can't even imagine.

All this DECEPTION, through a LIFETIME OF INDOCTRINATION, is held together by what you've been told is something called GRAVITY.

My beloved child, in my Word I reveal to you, but only when you have humbled yourself like a little child, my Word reveals to you, at the beginning of Genesis, that THE EARTH THAT I CREATED IS FLAT.

My Word tells you that "The earth was without form and void, and darkness was upon the face of the deep, and my Spirit moved upon THE FACE OF THE WATERS".

My beloved child, what SURFACE do you see with ANY BODY OF WATER?

Whether you are looking at your bath full of water, a stream, a river, a lake, a reservoir, an ocean... THAT BODY OF WATER IS FLAT.

THE EARTH THAT I CREATED IS FLAT.

My beloved child, my Word tells you that the earth that I created, DOES NOT SPIN AND IS NOT FLYING THROUGH WHAT YOU HAVE BEEN TOLD IS THE UNIVERSE.

My Word tells you in 1 Chronicles 16, that "The WORLD also shall be STABLE, THAT IT BE NOT MOVED".

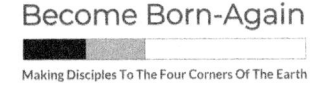

My Word tells you in Psalm 93 verse 1, "The WORLD also is established, THAT IT CANNOT BE MOVED".

Oh my beloved child, HUMBLE YOURSELF.

You have been deceived throughout your entire life.

My Word tells you in Colossians 2 verse 8, "Beware lest any man spoil you through philosophy and vain deceit, after the tradition of men, after the rudiments of the world, and not after me, the Lord of lords, the King of kings, the one given the name above all names.

I AM the Alpha and the Omega.

I AM the First and the Last.

I AM the beginning and the end.

I AM the resurrection and the life, and I AM A JEALOUS GOD, and I will not allow you my beloved child to be deceived by man any longer.

Humble yourself like a little child. No longer be afraid to tell other people that the earth that I created, I the one true living God, is FIXED, IMMOVABLE, it will not be moved and that THE EARTH THAT I CREATED IS FLAT. YOU DO NOT LIVE ON A SPINNING GLOBE FLYING THROUGH WHAT YOU HAVE BEEN TOLD IS "THE UNIVERSE".

Now GO.

Continue to OBLITERATE powers and principalities of darkness.

Continue to SPEAK MY WORD.

Continue to DECLARE MY WORD.

Continue to STAND ON MY WORD.

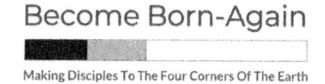

CONTINUE TO BE MY HANDS AND FEET, for I have called YOU by name from your mother's womb to be one of my increasing army of glory carriers - men, women and children who I the Lord your God are anointing to do even greater things than I did. Yes, ALL MY PROMISES, through my Word from the start of Genesis to the end of Revelation, are yes and amen, IN MY PERFECT TIME.

Look around at the nations. Look and be amazed! In all your days, have you ever seen anything like this? I AM doing something in your own day, something you wouldn't even believe even if someone told you about it.

IN ALL YOUR HISTORY, have you ever seen anything like this before? Tell your children about it in the years to come, and tell your children to tell their children. PASS THE STORY DOWN OF MY WORLDWIDE REFORMATION FROM GENERATION TO GENERATION.

And remember my beloved child, my Word in Ecclesiastes 3 verses 14 to 15, "Whatever I the King of Glory do is final. Nothing can be added to it or taken from it. My purpose is that men should be fearful before me, to have reverent fear of me, for I hold EVERYONE in the palm of my hand, I SUSTAIN ALL LIFE.

What you are experiencing now, what I began doing in the early part of 2020, has happened before and what will happen in the future has happened before, because I the Lord of lords, the King of kings, the one given the name above all names, I MAKE THE SAME THINGS HAPPEN OVER AND OVER AGAIN.

My beloved child, no longer hold back from telling those who are lost, those who are in captivity, those who are still deceived, that the earth that I created is fixed, immovable and it is flat, says I the Sovereign Lord.

September 20th 2022

I Am Imploring You To Accept That I Truly Do Work In ALL THINGS For Good, Says The Lord

My beloved, I am calling you to no longer give your time, energy and words to things which are from a place of sin, of darkness, of deception, of fear, of evil.

My beloved, I am imploring you to focus on things above not things below. I am imploring you to accept that I TRULY DO WORK IN ALL THINGS FOR GOOD for those who love me and those who live according to my purpose for them.

I am imploring you to praise me, to worship me, to speak to me, to hear from me EACH DAY. My beloved, the more that you focus your mind and your heart on me and my Word, the less that you are focusing on the situations and circumstances and experiences in your life and those things taking place across the earth.

There is power in your tongue, to speak life or to speak death. My Word is life. Speak life. Read my Word. Declare my Word. Use my name. I have been given the name above all names.

My beloved, let go of being consumed by things taking place on the earth. I AM IN CONTROL. I AM SOVEREIGN. Let go of everything. Let go of all your burdens, cast your burdens upon me because I care for you.

As you are receiving my words to you now, I'm destroying the yokes of bondage that have been in your life.

I am destroying the chains to your past.

I am destroying the spirits that have been causing you to focus on things taking place in your life, the spirits that have been keeping you in your flesh.

I am destroying the strongmen that have held you in prison, in iron bars.

My beloved, don't look left, don't look right, don't look behind you, look straight ahead to fix your eyes on me, because I am the author and the finisher of your faith and MY WAY IS PERFECT, so when you focus on me, you are focusing on my perfect way, you are focusing your time, your energy, your attention and your heart and your desires on my way, which is perfect.

I am the one that makes a way in the wilderness.

I am the one that takes your ashes and turns them into beauty.

I am the one that takes your pains and turns them into your testimony.

I am the one that turns your darkness into my glorious light.

I am the one that has you in the palm of my hand.

My beloved, I have called you by name from your mother's womb to be my glory carrier. To walk each day and to live in joy and peace. To walk each day by faith and not by sight. To put your trust in me and in me alone. To lean not on your own understanding. My beloved, I AM IMPLORING YOU to give me EVERYTHING, to surrender EVERYTHING in your life to me.

My beloved, to me the darkness and the light are the same. I WORK IN ALL THINGS IN YOUR LIFE FOR GOOD, because you love me, because you live according to my purpose for you, and as I am establishing right now, deep in your heart my purpose for you, my beloved, you are receiving now by my Spirit, that my purpose for you is to glorify and worship me each day, to have a thankfulness, a gratefulness and a joy in your heart each day from when you wake up in the morning, because my beloved, you always have something to be joyful for, because you have my breath in your lungs. You have my breath in your lungs. I sustain you, my beloved, in spite of what's been going on in your life, you are here today receiving my words because of my grace for you, because of my mercy for you, because of my unfailing love for you.

My beloved, your eyes have not yet seen, your ears have not yet heard in your mind has not yet conceived what I the Lord your God have got planned for you because you love me.

No longer give time, energy and words to darkness, to evil, to fear.

May my Word be on your tongue throughout each day.

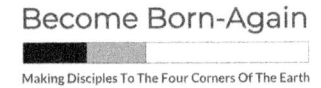

The more that you saturate your eye gates and your ear gates and your heart and your mind with the things of my kingdom, the more of my glory will be coming into your life, because I am the King of glory, and I have called you by name, my beloved, to be my glory carrier, says either Sovereign Lord.

For I know the plans I have for you," says the LORD. "They are plans for good and not for disaster, to give you a future and a hope. In those days when you pray, I will listen. If you look for me wholeheartedly, you will find me. I will be found by you," says the LORD. "I will end your captivity and restore your fortunes. I will gather you out of the nations where I sent you and will bring you home again to your own land."

Jeremiah 29:11-14

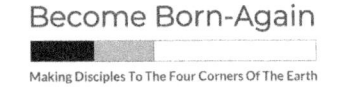

RELATIONSHIP

Start living in a deepening, intimate, life-changing relationship with Jesus

And we know that God causes everything to work together for the good of those who love God and are called according to his purpose for them. For God knew his people in advance, and he chose them to become like his Son, so that his Son would be the firstborn among many brothers and sisters.

Romans 8:28-29

You must have the same attitude that Christ Jesus had. Though he was God, he did not think of equality with God as something to cling to. Instead, he gave up his divine privileges; he took the humble position of a slave and was born as a human being. When he appeared in human form,
he humbled himself in obedience to God and died a criminal's death on a cross.

Philippians 2:5-8

Since God chose you to be the holy people he loves, you must clothe yourselves with tenderhearted mercy, kindness, humility, gentleness, and patience.

Colossians 3:12

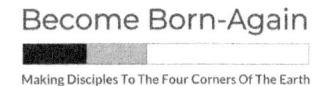

But the Holy Spirit produces this kind of fruit in our lives: love, joy, peace, patience, kindness, goodness, faithfulness, gentleness, and self-control.
There is no law against these things!

Galatians 5:22-23

But Jesus said, "Let the children come to me. Don't stop them! For the Kingdom of Heaven belongs to those who are like these children."

Matthew 19:14

January 20th 2023

Truly, Truly, Truly Become Like A Little Child, Says The Lord

My beloved child, my Word tells you that my Kingdom belongs to those who are like little children. My Word also tells you that unless you turn from your sins and become like little children, you will never get into my Kingdom.

My beloved child, I am imploring you now, for the first time in your life, to truly, truly become like a little child.

I am imploring you to LET GO COMPLETELY OF EVERY SINGLE THING YOU HAVE BEEN TOLD, YOU HAVE BEEN TAUGHT, YOU HAVE BEEN SUBJECTED TO, BY SINFUL, DECEITFUL MAN. This includes BOTH those who I haven't yet set free and those who I have already brought into a relationship with me.

My beloved child, HUMBLE YOURSELF.

No longer allow things that you have been taught by man to override my Word.

I have put my Spirit into you, and greater is the spirit that is in you than the spirit that is in the world, AND MY SPIRIT IS YOUR TEACHER.

TRULY BECOME LIKE A LITTLE CHILD, but whereas when you were a little child walking the earth, with your innocence, you trusted what people in your life taught you, but now my beloved, as you now become like a little child, I have given you the eyes to see and the ears to hear my voice and to receive wisdom and revelation every single day, from my Word, by My Spirit, from the throne room.

I the Lord am a jealous God. I am a devouring fire, and I have seen ENOUGH of my people living with pride.

I have seen enough of my people living in bondage, in slavery, being oppressed by the Leviathan spirit, but I the Lord, by my sword, I AM THE ONE THAT DESTROYS LEVIATHAN.

I AM THE ONE THAT DESTROYS JEZEBEL.

I AM THE ONE THAT DESTROYS THE ANTICHRIST SPIRIT.

My beloved child, live your life worthy of the calling that you have received.

I have called you by name from your mother's womb to be my hands and feet, to be one of my glory carriers.

I have called you by name to truly become like a little child, and to crave pure spiritual milk from my Word, by my Spirit.

No longer rely on any man or woman in your life or that will come into your life to be your teacher. My Spirit is your teacher, today and for the rest of your days serving me upon the earth, says I the Sovereign Lord.

September 14th 2022

Now Is The Time To Make Me The Lord Over Your ENTIRE Life, Says The Lord

My beloved, it is now time to make me, the Lord, over your ENTIRE LIFE.

Make me the Lord over your whole body.

Make me the Lord over your thoughts.

Make me the Lord over your feelings.

Make me the Lord over your tongue.

Make me the Lord over your entire family.

Make me the Lord over every single one of your relationships.

Make me the Lord over the work that you do.

Make me the Lord of your decisions.

Make me the Lord of where you go.

Make me the Lord over what words you speak.

Make me the Lord of your finances.

Make me the Lord over your entire life.

My beloved, no longer love the things of the world in ANY WAY.

No longer hold back from sharing your faith in me, as you don't want to cause offence.

No longer hide away from speaking about me to complete strangers.

No longer say "I can't do this", "I can't do that", "I'm no good at that", "I've never been good at that".

SPEAK MY WORD INTO EVERY AREA OF YOUR LIFE.

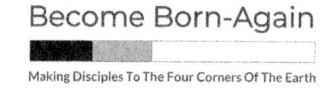

Speak a prophetic word into those things in your life which currently appear to be dead and buried. Ask me the Lord your God to breathe my breath of life into the areas of your life, which may currently seem impossible.

Remember, what is impossible with man is possible with me.

May 7th 2022

It Is Time For You To Let Go Of All Remaining Inhibitions, Says The Lord

My beloved child, I am calling you to let go of all remaining inhibitions. Inhibitions which have held you back from coming into an intimate relationship with Me. Inhibitions which have been a part of your life, which have been a part of your old self, your old wineskins. I am calling you to worship me in spirit and in truth and when you are listening to anointed worship music on your own, in private, I am calling you to lift your arms to the air, to allow me to pour into you my spirit, for me to release an anointing upon you that will bring you into tears, and through this anointing , through me filling you with my spirit as you release and let go of all your inhibitions, you will begin to hear from me more clearly than you ever have done before.

You are the apple of my eye. You are my masterpiece. I know everything about you. Every moment of your entire life was laid out before a single day had passed, including this moment right now as you are receiving my words to you.

My call to you, to let go of all inhibitions, to let go of the shackles that have held you back from truly surrendering your entire life to me, inhibitions which have held you back from speaking about me, from talking about my goodness, speaking about how I have moved in your life, how I have carried you through all the darkest valleys of your entire life. But now as you open your heart more and more to me, as you worship me in spirit and in truth unlike you ever have done before, you will see that my presence, my spirit, will be upon you and immersing you unlike you have experienced before. And so I'm preparing you now, I'm preparing you now to be weeping tears of joy as you hear my voice more clearly than ever before.

And my beloved sons and daughters, your eyes haven't seen, your ears haven't heard and your minds haven't conceived what I the Lord your God have got planned for you because you love me.

Remember, greater is the spirit that is in you than the spirit that is in the world. I have called you by name, and you can do all things through me who give you strength. It isn't your will that will be done in your life, it is my will.

Let go of all your inhibitions. Open yourself up to come into a deepening, personal, intimate relationship with me the Lord your God. The more of me in your life, the less of you, and the more of me in your life, the more of my glory you will experience, because I am the King of Glory.

Thank you for receiving my words to you. You are the apple of my eye, says I the Lord of Heavens Armies.

May 19th 2023

May You NEVER AGAIN Live With Shyness, With Timidity, With Fear, Says The Lord

My beloved child, I am giving you wisdom and revelation of how I desire for you to live your life worthy of the calling that you have received.

I have called YOU by name from your mother's womb to be one of my chosen people.

I have chosen YOU to be one of my disciples.

I have chosen YOU to be one of my glory carriers.

I have chosen YOU to be my hands and feet

My Word tells you that if you are lukewarm, neither cold or hot, I will vomit you out of my mouth.

My Word tells you that it is a sin to know what you ought to do and then not do it.

My beloved child, my Word tells you that you should not be ashamed of the gospel, because it is a power of me the Lord your God that brings salvation to everyone who believes in me.

My beloved, the harvest is ready, but the workers are few, but you may ask, "But WHERE is the harvest?"

My beloved child, the HARVEST IS EVERY SINGLE PLACE THAT YOU GO IN YOUR DAY TO DAY LIFE.

THE HARVEST IS EVERYWHERE.

My beloved, if you confess me upon the earth before men, I will also confess you before my Father who is in heaven, but IF YOU DENY ME ON EARTH before men, you also I WILL ALSO DENY before my Father who is in heaven.

My beloved child, MAY THERE BE NO MORE TIMIDITY IN YOUR LIFE.

May there be NO MORE FEAR.

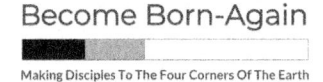

May there be NO MORE APPREHENSION.

May there be NO MORE HESITATION in telling complete strangers about me, about my love for that person.

EVERY SINGLE DAY I GIVE YOU OPPORTUNITIES to tell people that you have never met before about me.

Remember, EVERY DAY OF YOUR LIFE is written in my book. Every single moment was laid out before a single day passed. Every single thing that happens to you every single time someone comes into your life, every time that you speak to someone, every time that you see someone, IT WAS WRITTEN BY ME.

So, from this moment going forward, following you receiving my words now, you know that you have opportunities to tell people that I love them during your day to day activities, every day of your life.

When you receive a phone call from someone you don't know.

When someone calls at your home that you do not know.

When you have to make a phone call and you are going to speak to someone that you haven't met before.

When you leave your home and you see people.

When you go to your local shop.

When you are walking on the street.

When you are at the supermarket.

When you are getting petrol.

When you are at the laundrette.

When you are in a pub.

When you are in a restaurant.

When you are at a fast food drive-through.

When you are at the bakers.

When you are at the doctors.

When you are at the hospital.

When you are at the dentist.

When you are at the car showroom.

When you are at your place of work.

When you are at the park.

When you're on the school run.

When you live your life every single day, knowing that it is not you that live but I the Lord that lives in you.

When you leave your front door knowing that YOU ARE MY HANDS AND FEET.

EVERY SINGLE DAY you have OPPORTUNITIES TO TELL PEOPLE THAT YOU DO NOT KNOW ABOUT ME, for you to shine light into their darkness. For you to say "Can I pray for you?"

My beloved child, there is no more excuse. There is no more timidity. I have had you in the refiners fire for over three years since the beginning of 2020.

NOW IS THE TIME for you to be one of my disciples.

NOW IS THE TIME for you to live your life worthy of the calling that you have received, and that is to be one of my chosen people, one of my GLORY CARRIERS, to be my hands and feet upon the earth. To bring MY GLORY into other people's lives, as you go into the lives of complete strangers to tell them about me. For you to NO LONGER BE ASHAMED OF THE GOSPEL, because it is the power of me, the Lord your God, that brings salvation to everyone who believes.

For everyone who calls on my name will be saved. But how can they call on me to save them if they do not believe in me? How can they believe in me unless they know about me? How will they know about me unless someone tells them? How will someone tell them unless they are sent? That is why the Scriptures say "How beautiful are the feet of messengers that bring Good News".

My beloved child, may you NEVER AGAIN HIDE YOUR LIGHT UNDER A BUSHEL.

May you NEVER AGAIN BE FEARFUL OF SHARING THE GOOD NEWS.

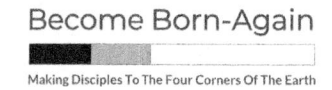

May you never again live with SHYNESS, with TIMIDITY, with FEAR.

I have NOT given you a spirit of fear, but of power, of love of a sound mind, and you are my beloved child, my hands and feet and my will be done in your life and in the lives of everyone walking the earth, on earth as it is in heaven, says I the Sovereign Lord.

February 13th 2023
They Don't Know, Says The Lord

My beloved child, you are receiving my message now, for I desire for you to have a greater understanding and a deeper comprehension of how I the Lord have prepared the harvest.

From you receiving my message, through the leading of my Spirit within you, I the Lord your God are going to be using you as my hands and feet, more and more and more.

The men, the women and the children whom I am going to be sending you into the life of DO NOT KNOW WHAT YOU KNOW.

They don't know of my unfailing love for them.

They don't know that I surrendered my life on the cross to save their life.

They don't know that I shed my blood on the cross so that they can be forgiven for all their sins.

They don't know that they have a spirit.

They don't know that their freedom comes only through having faith in me, the one given the name above all names.

They don't know that peace that I will give them is a gift the world cannot give them.

They don't know that it is only I the Lord your God that can free them from the pains of their past.

They don't know that it is only me that can free them from the trauma of their past.

They don't know that it is only me that can set them free from their guilt.

They don't know that it is only me that can set them free from their shame.

They don't know that it is only me that can destroy every chain of bondage that they are living with.

They don't know that it is only me that can take out of them their heart of stone and give them a new tender, responsive heart of flesh.

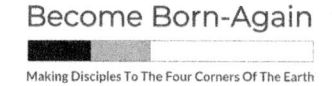

They don't know that it is only me by my Spirit and through their surrender to me that they can forgive those that they have been unable to forgive.

They don't know that if they don't repent and receive me as their Lord and Saviour, they will be going to hell.

They don't know they are chosen and not forsaken.

They don't know that once they resist the devil the devil will free from them.

They don't know that my perfect love expels all their fear.

They don't know that my peace surpasses all understanding, and it is going to guard their heart and mind.

They don't know that every day of their life is written in my book.

They don't know that every single moment of their lives was laid out before a single day have passed.

They don't know that my thoughts for them outnumber the grains of sand.

The men, the women and the children whom I the Lord are going to be sending you into the life of, don't yet know that they have been called by name from their mother's womb to become one of my disciples, to become one of my ever increasing glory carriers, to become like you, my beloved child, my hands and feet.

Look around my beloved child, THE HARVEST IS READY, and I have heard the prayers of my children, and I am sending more and more and more workers into the field.

My beloved child, your eyes have not seen, your ears have not heard and your mind has not yet conceived what I the Lord your God have got planned for you and all my chosen Sons and Daughters, because you love me.

Thank you, my beloved child, for receiving my message.

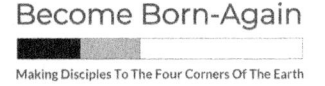

May 17th 2022

Be Content & Not Disappointed In ALL Your Circumstances, Says The Lord

My beloved, you are my masterpiece. I have called you by name. You are chosen and not forsaken. You are the apple of my eye. I am for you and not against you. My plans for your life are plans for good and not for disaster, to give you a future and a hope.

Please, my beloved, no longer be disappointed with anything that you experience in your life. Remember, every day of your life is written in my book, every single moment was laid out before a single day had passed.

Once you know that your identity is in me and in me alone, once you are completely surrendered to me, you have EVERYTHING that you need.

Every good gift and every perfect gift that has ever come into your life and that will ever come into your life is from my hand.

As I have called you by name, you have everything that you need.

As you seek My Kingdom and My righteousness first, everything else will be given unto you.

It is I the Lord your God that sent the locusts into your life and the locusts, the hopping locusts, the swarming locusts, the stripping locust have stripped you down and down and down. The locusts have been stripping away from you your old wineskins, your old habits, your old behaviours, your attachments to your past life experiences, relationships both short term and long term that no longer serve you, since you started following me, since you started hearing my voice.

Yes, the experiences that you've had during the last two years have been painful.

Yes, you have suffered.

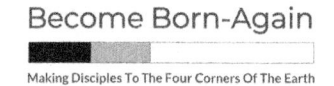

Yes, you have shed many, many tears, but through your suffering, through the trials, through the tribulations, through the dark valleys, through the storms, through the fiery furnace that you have been in, and that furnace has been getting hotter and hotter and hotter, it is I the Lord your God that have been in the furnace with you. Just like with Shadrach, Meshach and Abednego, I have been in the furnace with you, and my beloved in spite of what it has felt like, in spite of your life experiences taking you to a place of total brokenness, of feeling consumed, feeling overwhelmed, feeling surrounded on all sides, my beloved, it is I the Lord your God that have always surrounded you and I will always surround you with my mighty hand of protection, with my unfailing love.

My hand is mighty upon you, my beloved. No weapons that have been formed against you during your entire life have ever prospered. Your identity is in me and in me alone and through the fiery furnace that I have sent you through, I have been purifying you seven times over. I have used the locusts to utterly destroy your old wineskins, because I do not pour out my new wine, my new glory into your life. I do not pour out all my goodness and all my promises and all my breakthroughs and all my miracles, signs and wonders, I do not pour these into your life, when you were still living in your old wineskins, because your old self, your old identity, when you were living following the dictates of your sin nature, when you were a slave to your sin nature, when you were battling with your mind on your own, when you were committing sin, when you were living without a relationship with me - YOUR OLD SELF, YOUR OLD IDENTITY, WOULD NEVER, EVER HAVE BEEN ABLE TO COMPREHEND, TO EXPERIENCE AND TO LIVE WITH THE GLORY THAT I THE KING OF GLORY ARE PREPARING TO POUR OUT INTO YOUR LIFE.

I have chosen you, my beloved, to be my glory carrier. I have called you by name. Your eyes haven't seen, your ears haven't heard and your mind hasn't conceived what I the Lord your God have got planned for you, because you love me.

I am going to be showing you that I TRULY WORK IN ALL THINGS IN YOUR LIFE. Everything that you have ever experienced. I work in all things for your good because you love me and because you live according to my purpose for you.

My way is perfect. All my promises to you are yes and amen.

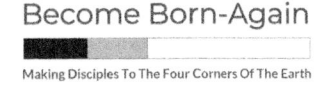

In my perfect time, those things that are on your heart right now, the things that I have placed upon your heart for the salvation of your loved ones, of your family, of the breakthroughs in your life, of the yearning that you have on your heart right now, for how you want to experience life and what you want to be doing, in my perfect time, the things on your heart will come to pass, says I the Lord of Heaven's Armies.

All my promises are yes and amen. My way is perfect, and you are my masterpiece.

My beloved, I am your provider. I meet ALL your needs. It is my breath in your lungs. You came into the world naked from your mother's womb and you will leave the earth naked. Everything that you have is because of me.

My beloved, I am calling you to be truly, truly content exactly where you are right now and exactly where I will take you, every single day moving forward for the rest of your life. Remember, my beloved, every day of your life is written in my book. I laid out every single moment of your entire life before a single day had passed. Please, my beloved. put your faith in me and in me alone, lean not on your own understanding. Be content with whatever circumstances I place you in. Know that even when you don't see it, I am working. Know that even when you don't feel it, I am working. I am the miracle worker and my beloved, with your faith in me and in me alone, with you surrendering your entire life to me, with your heart, truly, truly open to be in an intimate, personal deepening relationship with me, as I am now pouring more of My Spirit into you now, my beloved, YOU CAN PRAY FOR ANYTHING AND BECAUSE YOU HAVE FAITH, YOU WILL RECEIVE IT.

My beloved, may you never feel disappointed again. May you live a truly contented life filled with my Spirit, seeking me, being joyful and being glad in all your circumstances, worshipping me in spirit and in truth whether you are on the mountaintops or in the dark valleys, because remember, it is I the Lord your God who are with you every moment of your entire life. It is I the Lord your God that have brought you through every single trial and tribulation and suffering that you have ever experienced. I have seen every tear that you have ever shed, and I have caught them in my bottle, and my beloved, because you have sown with tears, you are going to reap with songs of joy.

Joy unlike you have ever experienced before is coming into your life.

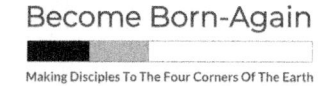

My peace is my gift to you that the world cannot give you, and my peace surpasses all understanding and it guards your heart and your mind in me, Christ Jesus, the Lord your God. I am the author and the finisher of your faith.

My way is perfect, and my plans for your life and your family are plans for good and not for disaster, to give you a future and a hope, says I the Lord of Heaven's Armies.

October 24th 2022

My Desire For You Is For You To Be Completely Surrendered To Me, Says The Lord

My beloved, my desire for you is for you to be completely surrendered to me.

My desire is that you have surrendered every single thing in your life to me.

Remember that I know and see everything.

I desire for you to be completely free.

I desire for your faith to be in me and in me alone.

I desire to answer your prayers.

My Word tells you in Matthew 7:7, "Ask and you will receive, seek and you will find, knock and the door will be open for you", but my Word also tells you that it is only my people with pure hearts and clean hands, that can climb my holy mountain. So my beloved, I am calling you now to go into the secret place, to get down onto your knees and to ask me, the Lord your God, to reveal to you what are the things that you haven't YET surrendered to me.

You will ask and you will receive, for I desire for you to know what it is you need to surrender to me. By my Spirit within you, I will speak to you and I will reveal to you what you need to surrender, and then through you surrendering that which you haven't previously surrendered, you will experience freedom. You will feel a burden lifted off you. The remaining chains to experiences that you've had in your past and things in your life currently, every chain is going to break in my name.

My promise to you my beloved child, is that you are no longer going to be weighed down. You are no longer going to be heavy laden. You are no longer going to be burdened with those things which you have been carrying, those things which you haven't previously surrendered to me.

I have called you by name from your mother's womb to be totally surrendered to me, for when you are totally surrendered to me, you are ready to truly receive everything that I've been preparing to pour into your life.

Remember my beloved, it is my breath in your lungs. It is I the Lord your God that sustain you. Your identity is not in the accumulation of things that you've experienced in your life. Your identity is not in those particular things that you've been holding on to, those things which you are going to be surrendering to me.

My beloved child, your identity is in me the Lord your God and in me alone.

From you receiving my message to you now, once you go into the secret place to come to me to ask me to reveal to you what you need to surrender to me, once you have surrendered those things, once you have experienced the chains breaking, once you have experienced the burden being lifted, my beloved child, I'm calling you to testify, to testify about what you experience. For your testimony is going to encourage more of your brothers and sisters that they too also need to come to me into the secret place, and ask me to reveal to them what they need to surrender to me.

Thank you, my beloved, for hearing my voice.

You are my masterpiece, says I the Lord your God.

May 7th 2022

I Am Calling You To Let Go Of All Control Of All Circumstances In Your Life, Says The Lord

My beloved child, I am calling you to completely surrender everything in your life. I am calling you to let go of all control of all the circumstances of your life, and also to let go of all your family members and all your loved ones whom I haven't yet removed the scales from their eyes.

This is going to be incredibly challenging for you, but through your total surrender, by you completely giving up ALL CONTROL of every single part of your entire life, this will allow me to work and move in your life in ways that will leave you breathless.

Through you giving up all control, you are showing that you trust in me completely. You are showing me that your faith is in me the Lord your God and in me alone. You will be showing me that you are willing to lean not on your own understanding, but instead trust in me and in my way because my way is perfect.

I am giving you the key now for you to unlock doors in your life that no man can shut, and by unlocking these doors, by you giving up all control, you will begin seeing breakthroughs in your life unlike you have experienced before.

Remember, my beloved child, my ways are higher than your ways and my thoughts are more than anything that you can imagine, just as the heavens are higher than the earth, my ways are higher than your ways.

Even when you don't see it, I am working. Even when you don't feel it, I am working. I want you to know that I am working in the hearts and minds of everyone that you have been praying for. Everyone that you have been interceding for, I am working.

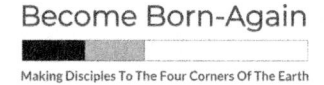

Surrender everything and everyone in your life to me. Let go and let me do what I have planned to do in your life, and in the lives of all your loved ones. All my promises are yes and amen, and you know that the testing of your faith produces perseverance, so let your perseverance grow.

I am perfecting your patience, as you trust in me, as you surrender to me, you are learning more and more, to live with patience, to trust me completely.

Thank you, my beloved child, for hearing my words to you, for receiving my words and for applying my words to you in your life from this moment forward. Your eyes haven't seen, your ears haven't heard and your minds haven't conceived what I the Lord your God, have got planned for you, because you love me.

Remember, my will be done on earth as it is in heaven, in your life, and in the lives of every single one of your loved ones, who may plan all kinds of things, but my will is going to be done, says I, the Lord of Heavens Armies.

October 14th 2022

I Am Continually Speaking To You, Says The Lord

My beloved, throughout your life I have been speaking to you. My desire is for you to know that throughout every day of your life moving forward, it is I the Lord your God that are in constant continual conversation with you. It takes place in your mind, so you don't hear my voice audibly, but it is I the Lord that is communicating to you in your mind, and the biggest reason that so often you haven't realised that it is I the Lord that is speaking to you, is because you haven't trusted that yes I am, continually speaking to you.

From the smallest, most insignificant moments of your life through to the greatest, through to the biggest, through to the most challenging, through to the moments in your life when suddenly your circumstances change, my beloved, from you receiving my message to you now, you will have the discernment to know that I am speaking to you, that I am guiding you, that I am strengthening you, that I am supporting you, that I am bringing you peace, that I am bringing you clarity, that I am taking away any possible confusion, because what I am doing inside of you, my beloved, I am continuing to build up your faith in me. I am continuing to bring you into a more deeper, in a more personal, in a more life changing relationship with me the Lord your God.

My beloved, smile, smile because I'm speaking to you now, through you receiving my words. You are going to be smiling as you have more than ever before in your life, absolute complete clarity when I'm speaking to you and that you are in conversation with me in your mind, and in these conversations that you will be having with me in your mind, I will be helping you and guiding you and giving you understanding and wisdom and revelation of what is taking place in your life.

My beloved, before I created the heavens and the earth, I planned for you to be receiving my message to you now, because I have planned for you for the rest of your life to be in continual conversation with me in your mind.

Be prepared my beloved, for me to bring you into tears. Tears because you are receiving my words to you more than ever before. Tears because your life is going to start becoming truly profound. Tears because I am giving you greater and greater comprehension of have how much I love you, because you my beloved are my masterpiece, says I the Sovereign Lord.

September 24th 2022

You Are Going To Be Hearing My Voice More Clearly And More Regularly Than You Have Ever Experienced Before, Says The Lord

My beloved, from you receiving my message to you now, you are going to be hearing my voice more clearly and more regularly than you have ever experienced before.

There are particular words that you are going to be hearing me say to you.

You are going to hear me say to you "Remember, it is ALL written", when you are faced with a challenging situation or circumstance or the behaviour of someone in your life. "Remember, it is ALL written".

You are going to hear me say to you "Keep trusting me" as you are beginning to be drawn into your feelings and your emotions, when things in your life don't go the way that you're expecting them or are hoping them to. "Keep trusting me".

I am going to bring you into tears of praise and worship, when I say to you "I told you I would do it". ALL my promises to you are yes and amen. I know your heart's desires, because it is I the Lord your God that have placed those desires upon your heart, and in my perfect time, you will see that I will answer your prayer, and you will be crying tears of breakthrough, tears of awe and wonder, tears because you hear me say to you "I told you I would do it".

You are also going to hear me speak to you to bring you subtle but important correction each day, at moments when you are being drawn into your flesh and you are developing negative feelings or emotions. You will hear me say to you:

"Stop moaning"

"Stop complaining"

"Stop getting frustrated"

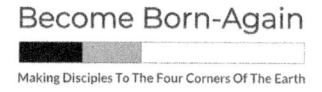

"Stop judging".

"Stop trying to fight this battle".

You will hear me say to you "This battle belongs to me", and you will surrender that that is taking place in your life to me.

You will hear me say to you "I am in total control" when the circumstances of your life make you feel like things are going out of control.

You will hear me say to you "I am with you, keep trusting me" as you enter into a situation or a circumstance where you would have normally felt disturbed, frustrated, worried or concerned.

My beloved, the words that you are going to hear me speak to you which will have the greatest impact on your trust and your faith in me, is when I say to you, "I told you I would do it".

My beloved, I am calling you to not just walk by faith, not by sight, but also to talk by faith, not by sight.

Speak about my promises to you.

Speak about the salvation of your loved ones, which hasn't YET happened.

Speak about those things that are on your heart right now, that haven't YET come to pass.

Walk by faith and talk by faith, and be prepared to hear me speak to you more and more and more throughout each day, as you are truly desiring to be in a deepening, intimate, personal relationship with me, the Lord your God.

June 27th 2023

Read My Word Whilst Praying In Tongues, Says The Lord

My beloved child, **I desire to continually give you wisdom and revelation by my Spirit.**

My Word tells you to call on me and I will answer, to ask me and I will tell you great and marvellous things, secrets you do not know.

My Word tells you that my ways are higher than your ways, and my thoughts are more than anything that you can think or imagine, just as the heavens are higher than the earth.

My Word tells you that if you need wisdom, to ask me and I will tell you, for I am generous, and I will not rebuke you for asking me for wisdom. But when you ask me, **to make sure that your faith is in me, and in me alone.**

My beloved child, you know that **there are nine gifts of my Spirit.**

You know that my Word from the beginning of Genesis to the end of Revelation is alive and active, sharper than the sharpest two-edged sword.

My Word tells you that **Paul prayed in tongues more than anyone.**

You know that **love should be your highest goal, but that you should also desire the special abilities that my Spirit gives, especially the ability to prophesy.**

My beloved child, I am sharing something with you now that **so few of my people walking the earth have been doing.**

As you read my Word, pray in tongues.

When you do this, you will realise that you are still able to read my Word and take in my Word and to be fed by my Word, whilst you are praying in tongues.

In addition, my beloved child, because you are praying in tongues, because you are speaking by the power of my Spirit, and because you are talking only to me, you will start to **experience me giving you wisdom and revelation through my Word** in a way which you haven't experienced before.

By my Spirit **you will receive revelation** as you read my Word, filled with my Spirit, praying to me and speaking to me in tongues.

Not only will I be strengthening you personally, you will find that all the gifts of my Spirit such as **words of knowledge**, **words of wisdom and in particular prophecy,** will be getting stirred up on the inside of you.

My beloved child, **I desire for you to harness and to experience all the gifts of my Spirit.**

I desire to take you deeper in your relationship with me.

I desire to draw you closer to me.

I desire to give you wisdom and revelation each day.

I desire for you every day to deny yourself, to pick up your cross daily and follow me.

My beloved child, I am taking you deeper.

I am taking you to a place where your faith is unlike you have ever experienced before.

I am drawing you closer to me, so that my Word comes alive in your spirit more and more and more.

My beloved child, you will do the same things that I have done and even greater things. You will be able to say to a mountain may be lifted up and thrown to the sea, and because you have faith and do not doubt it, because you have the gift of faith, **it will happen.**

Remember, my Word tells you in Matthew 21 22, "You can pray for anything, and if you have faith, you will receive it."

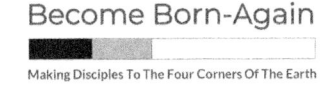

Read my Word whilst praying in tongues, and what you speak after and what you pray for after, will be words and prayers that in my time, when I answer your prayers, **will leave you breathless,** says I the Sovereign Lord.

May 30th 2022

Listen To My Voice & My Will For Your Life Above Anyone In Your Life, Says The Lord

My beloved, I have called you by name to be my glory carrier. My beloved, as I am pouring into you my spirit, I am truly setting you on fire.

My beloved, it is completely irrelevant that you have only been walking with me for a short period of time. I am pouring into you wisdom that I haven't provided to my people who have been walking with me for years and years and years and years. I am pouring into you wisdom and revelation because of your true and complete surrender to me. As you have been willing to completely die to your flesh, as you have been willing to pick up your cross and follow me, as you have been willing to become an enemy of the world in order to follow my leading, I am now repaying you with wisdom and secrets that I have not shared with those who have been seeking me for years and years and years.

My beloved, my call to you now is to not allow any of your brothers or your sisters to quench my Spirit that I am pouring into you each day.

My beloved, seek me, seek my voice and SEEK WISDOM FROM ME ABOVE ANY MAN OR WOMAN WALKING THE EARTH.

Be prepared for resistance.

Be prepared to have people in your life questioning what you are doing.

Be prepared for those closest to you to try and put an end to what I am calling you to do.

Be prepared for resistance, but know this my beloved, in the resistance that I am bringing into your life, I am refining you by fire. I am preparing you to impact the kingdom of darkness, unlike you can even comprehend.

My beloved, your eyes haven't seen, your ears haven't heard and your mind hasn't conceived what I the Lord your God have got planned for you because you love me.

RESIST THE RESISTANCE OF MAN.

Step off the boat in faith.

Go out with a Holy boldness.

Go through the doors that I am opening up in your life.

Don't try to open the doors that I have been shutting in your life.

Follow my will each day.

Hear my voice each day.

Seek my Kingdom and my righteousness first each day, and my beloved, all else will be given on to you.

In my Kingdom, says I the Lord of Heaven's Armies, the duration of which my chosen Sons and Daughters have been walking with me is completely irrelevant, in relation to the impact that they are going to have for My Kingdom, for My glory, because I am the King of glory, and my beloved, I have chosen you, yes you, to be my glory courier, says I the Lord of Heaven's Armies.

February 6th 2023

My Beloved Child, Can You Now See The Significance Of Your Purpose On Earth, Says The Lord

My beloved child, before I created the heavens and the earth, I planned and I ordained for you to receive my message to you now.

As you are receiving my words, my Spirit is upon you. I have put my Spirit in you and greater is the Spirit that is in you than the spirit that is in the world.

I am giving you WISDOM, UNDERSTANDING and COMPREHENSION of the SIGNIFICANCE, of the IMPORTANCE, of YOUR PURPOSE on earth alongside every single one of my chosen Sons and Daughters.

For hundreds of years, a gross darkness has covered the earth.

I have allowed for an increasing amount of sin to pollute the earth.

Over hundreds of years, ALL AREAS OF SOCIETY, INCLUDING MY CHURCH, have been polluted by sin.

For hundreds of years, there has been a FAMINE of my Word, of my living Word.

Over hundreds of years, I have allowed sin and iniquity to run through families across multiple generations.

Generation after generation there has been abuse.

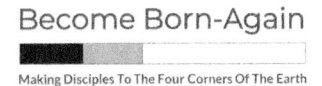

Generation after generation there has been addictions.

Generation after generation there has been health issues.

Generation after generation there has been mental health affliction.

Generation after generation there has been demonic possession.

Generation after generation there has been demonic oppression.

Generation after generation there has been marital breakdown.

Generation after generation there has been sin and iniquity.

My beloved, fearfully and wonderfully made child, since the start of the year 2020, men, women and children across the entire stationery earth that I created have started to comprehend that they have been LIED TO, that they have been DECEIVED, that they have been INDOCTRINATED, through their entire life, and through the lives of their parents and grandparents.

In all your history, HAVE YOU EVER SEEN ANYTHING LIKE THIS BEFORE?

I, the Lord of lords, the King of kings, the Alpha and the Omega, the beginning and the end, the first and the last, I AM SHAKING EVERYTHING THAT CAN BE SHAKEN.

THE REASON that your life your circumstances, your relationships, your feelings, your emotions, have been so intensely challenging and at times almost unbearable, is because you my beloved are living in and through, and becoming an increasingly important and influential part of, MY WORLDWIDE REFORMATION.

I am simultaneously setting my chosen people FREE.

I am simultaneously SHAKING people who are connected together.

I am simultaneously using my Sons and Daughters to absolutely OBLITERATE GENERATIONAL CURSES.

I am simultaneously using my Sons and Daughters to absolutely OBLITERATE ANCESTRAL CURSES.

I am simultaneously using my Sons and Daughters to absolutely OBLITERATE GENERATIONAL CYCLES OF ABUSE.

I am simultaneously using my Sons and Daughters to absolutely OBLITERATE GENERATIONAL CYCLES OF ADDICTION.

I am simultaneously using my Sons and Daughters to absolutely OBLITERATE STRONGMEN that have had a hold of families across generations.

I am simultaneously using my Sons and Daughters to send my Word out, and when I send my Word out, it does not return to me void. It accomplishes all that I desire and it prospers EVERYWHERE that I send it.

I am simultaneously bringing about FAMILY RECONCILIATION.

I am simultaneously SANCTIFYING my Sons and Daughters in the refiners fire, yes, my beloved, including you.

I am simultaneously setting the captives FREE.

I am simultaneously giving my chosen people the EYES TO SEE AND EARS TO HEAR.

I am simultaneously LIFTING THE VEIL on more and more men, women and children.

I am simultaneously POURING MY SPIRIT OUT upon my chosen people.

I am simultaneously SEPARATING out the wheat from the chaff.

My beloved child, CAN YOU NOW SEE THE SIGNIFICANCE OF YOUR LIFE?

Can you now see how precious you are to me?

Can you now see, that I the Lord have carried you through every dark valley, that I the Lord have been in the fire with you like Shadrach, Meshach and Abednego, and in spite of the intensity, in spite of the crushing, in spite of the pressing, in spite of you feeling surrounded on all sides, through all of what you've been experiencing, I the Lord your God have been sanctifying you.

I am purifying you.

I am moulding you more and more and more into my image.

Yes, it is I the Lord that has sent locusts into your life, and the locusts have been destroying everything that has been a part of your old self.

Your old habits.

Your old behaviours.

Your old thought patterns.

Your old belief systems.

Your old relationships.

Your old characteristics.

Your old personality traits.

Your old self.

I have been creating in you, my beloved child, YOUR NEW WINESKINS.

I the Lord your God have put my Spirit into you, and I am taking out of you now your heart of stone, and from my throne room I am giving you now a new, tender, responsive heart of flesh.

My beloved child, your identity is no longer in ANYTHING from your past.

Your identity is in me the Lord your God and in me alone.

I have given you a new heart, and I have created in you your new wineskins.

Your identity is in me, and now my beloved child, from you receiving my message, I can now truly begin to pour out new wine into your life in ways in which you have never experienced before.

My beloved child, your eyes have not seen, your ears have not heard and your mind has not yet conceived what I the Lord your God have got planned for you because you love me.

Remember, you are not trying to win the approval of people, but of me, the Lord your God, the one who created you, the one who sustains you. If pleasing people were your goal, you will not be my servant.

Remember my beloved child, it is not you that live but I that live in you.

You can do and you will do all things through me the Lord your God, who gives you strength.

My will be done, on earth as it is in heaven, in your life and in the lives of every man, woman and child walking the earth and who will walk the earth forevermore, says I the Sovereign Lord.

January 17th 2023

Never, Ever Underestimate The IMPACT That You Can Have, Says The Lord

My beloved child, the more that I have opened your eyes to the scale and depth of sin, of lies, of corruption, of deception, of indoctrination across the earth, you have had times when you have felt overwhelmed and helpless to make a change within the world.

The thought has come into your mind:

"What can I really do to make a difference?"

"How can just me on my own make an impact?"

My beloved child, you are receiving my message right now, for I planned and ordained for this moment before I created the heavens and the earth.

Not only have I started a fire deep down inside of you, a burning desire to read my Word, to know me, to speak to me, to seek me, to worship me, to be in fellowship with your on fire brothers and sisters, not only is it what I am doing on the inside of you my beloved child, but my message to you now is that I am going to be using you to be a FIRE STARTER in the lives of other people whom you haven't yet met.

I am going to be using you to go into the lives of people you haven't yet met, to speak a word of wisdom, a word of knowledge, and to offer prayers for someone who I have been preparing, who I have been building up on the inside of them, TO ALL OF A SUDDEN HAVE AN ENCOUNTER WITH YOU, and I'm going to use you to be the FIRE STARTER. I am going to use YOU to set that person on fire, with your words of truth, with your words of prayer.

My beloved child, it is not about you. It is not about what you think you can and can't do. It is about what I the Lord can do and will do through you, for I have put my spirit into you, and greater is the spirit that is in you than the spirit that is in the world, and my beloved child, YOU CAN DO AND YOU WILL DO ALL THINGS THROUGH ME THE LORD YOUR GOD WHO GIVES YOU STRENGTH.

Never, ever, underestimate the impact that you can have when you serve me, when you are my hands and feet.

Remember the impact across the world both then and now of one man, the Apostle Paul.

NEVER, EVER UNDERESTIMATE THE IMPACT THAT YOU CAN HAVE.

Never underestimate what I can do with ANYONE.

I am going to be giving you divine appointments.

I am going to be speaking to you.

I am going to be bringing conviction upon your heart to go over to that person that you have never met before, to speak to them, to share my love, to share the Gospel, to share your testimony, to offer to pray for them, to share with them that they have been called by name from their mother's womb to be one of my glory carriers just like you, my beloved child.

As you are receiving my words right now, the fire, the fire, the fire of my Spirit is falling upon you. I am truly setting you on fire.

MY DEVOURING FIRE IS GOING TO BE IN YOU AND COMING THROUGH YOU as you speak my Word, as you declare my Word, as you decree my Word. But not only this, my beloved child, I am going to be using you to set my chosen sons and daughters on fire.

Now go, serve me. Ask me "How can I serve you today Lord?".

Be my hands and feet.

Be my disciple.

Be one of my growing army of glory carriers, says I THE Sovereign Lord.

February 5th 2023

Remember, You Are Not Trying To Win The Approval Of People, But Of Me, Says The Lord

My beloved child, I have called you by name to live in freedom.

From when you began to speak about me the Lord your God, you started to receive negative words, negative behaviour and negative actions from people in your life - people who I haven't yet set free.

People who deny me and who live their life in sin have at times shown you total disrespect.

You have been mocked.

You have been slandered.

You have been told that you are deceived.

You have been hated by other people.

You have been judged.

You have been falsely accused.

You have received condemnation from other people.

You have received ALL OF THESE THINGS because you are my follower - you are my precious child.

You have experienced all of these things for my hand is mighty upon you, and I the Lord your God WORK IN ALL THINGS in your life for good, because you love me, because you live according to my purpose for you.

My beloved child, you have been in the refiners fire, and at times that fire has been getting hotter and hotter and hotter.

At times you have felt surrounded on all sides.

At times you have felt hounded by people.

You have been crushed.

You have been beaten down.

My beloved child, you have also experienced judgement, accusatory words, condemning words, mocking words, words aimed to bring doubt.

Words aimed to bring confusion from your own brothers and sisters who are in a relationship with me.

My beloved child, I am giving you wisdom now as to why I wrote for all these things to take place in your life, for every day of your life is written in my book, every single moment was laid out before a single day had passed.

My Word tells you in Galatians 1 verse 10, that you, my beloved child, are not trying to win the approval of people, but of me, the Lord your God. If pleasing people were your goal, you would not be my servant.

My beloved child, continue to live your life desiring to be in a deeper, in a more intimate personal relationship with me the Lord your God. My Word tells you in James 1 that if you need wisdom, to ask me for I am generous and I will give you wisdom, I will not rebuke you for asking, but ensure my beloved that YOUR FAITH IS IN ME AND IN ME ALONE. Have ZERO FAITH in anyone in your life.

By my Spirit, I will reveal to you when a brother or a sister is speaking into your life and it is from me, or whether it is from the enemy.

Remember, my Spirit is your teacher, and my Spirit will lead you into all truth.

Continue to share the truth in love.

I the Lord your God do not give wisdom and revelation at the same time to all my people.

The more humble you live your life in me the Lord your God, the more wisdom and revelation I will pour out to you.

Remember my beloved, with every one that has ever come against you and every one that will come against you moving forward, you do not fight against flesh and blood enemies, but against evil rulers and authorities of the unseen world, against mighty powers in this dark world and against evil spirits in the heavenly places.

Therefore, my beloved, put on every piece of my armour so you will be able to resist the enemy in the time of evil. Then after the battle, you will still be standing firm. Stand your ground, putting on the belt of truth and the body armour of my righteousness. For shoes, put on the peace that comes from the Good News so that you will be fully prepared. In addition to all of these, hold up the shield of faith, to stop the fiery arrows of the devil. Put on salvation as your helmet and take the sword of the Spirit which is my Word.

Thank you my beloved for receiving my message to you now.

Remember, you are not trying to win the approval of people, but of me the Lord your God. For if you are pleasing people, you will not be my servant, says I the Sovereign Lord.

May 27th 2022

I Have Chosen YOU To Be The 1st Through Your Entire Family Generations To Be My Glory Carrier, Says The Lord

My beloved, I want to give YOU a deep comprehension and a life-changing revelation of just how significant you are to me.

It was I the Lord your God that chose YOU before I created the Heavens and the earth. I planned out every single day of everyone that has ever lived in your family generational history. Every single moment was laid out before a single day had passed, and my beloved, I chose YOU to be the first throughout all your family generations to be given the true revelation, that you are, yes you my beloved, YOU ARE MY GLORY CARRIER.

I want you for a few moments to comprehend the life experiences that your family members have had by not being in relationship with me. Before I called you out of the darkness before I came down from Heaven and rescued you from all your enemies, before I saved you, you and all your current family members and those from generations past were and had lived in darkness, lived following the dictates of your sin nature, lived trying to win the battle of your mind and of your heart on your own, by your own strength.

My beloved, for a few moments, consider the battles that have gone on in your mind and in the lives of every single one of your family members. Fear. Anxiety. Depression. Anger. Bitterness. Resentment. Feeling helpless. Feeling hopeless. Feeling unloved. Unable to forgive those that have hurt you.

As I am pouring my spirit into you now, I am giving you a deeper revelation of the pain, the turmoil, the suffering, the battles that have raged in the lives of your entire family, those who are alive today and those that are no longer walking the earth.

Yes my beloved, I CHOSE YOU.

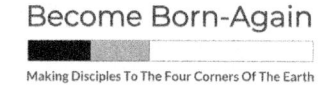

I chose to set YOU on fire with my Holy Spirit.

I chose YOU to come into the comprehension that your identity is in me, the Lord your God and in me along.

I chose YOU to be my glory carrier.

I chose to lift the veil from YOU.

I chose to remove the scales from YOUR eyes and not any one of your other family members.

YOU are the first but my beloved YOU WILL NOT BE THE LAST, says I the Lord of Heaven's Armies.

YOU are my anointed one. I am empowering your right hand. In the spirit realm, before YOU my beloved, mighty kings will be paralysed with fear. Their fortress gates will be opened, never to shut again. I will go before you my beloved and level the mountains. I will smash down gates of bronze and cut through bars of iron. Yes, my beloved, what is impossible with man is possible with me. Your family members alive today whom I haven't yet set free, I will set them free, says I the Lord of Heaven's Armies. I will lift the veil. I will remove the scales from their eyes, and my beloved, when I send my word out to you now, it does not return to me void, it will accomplish all that I desire and it prospers EVERYWHER that I send it.

My beloved, you yes you, ARE MY MASTERPIECE.

I am going to be giving you treasures hidden in the darkness. Secret riches.

Your eyes haven't seen, your ears haven't heard and your mind hasn't conceived what I the Lord your God have got planned for you, because you love me.

Everything that I am doing in your life and everything to come in your life, my beloved, I am doing all of this so that you may know that I am the Lord, the God of Israel, the one who calls YOU by name. And why have I called YOU, my beloved, for this work? Why did I call you by name when you did not know me? It is for the sake of Jacob my servant, Israel, my chosen one. I am the Lord, there is no other God.

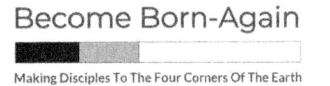

My beloved, I have equipped you for battle, though you don't even know me. So all the world from east to west will know there is no other God. I am the Lord and there is no other. I create the light and make the darkness. I send good times and bad times. I the Lord am the one who does these things. Open up oh heavens and pour out your righteousness. Let the earth open wide so salvation and righteousness can sprout up together. I the Lord created them.

My beloved, through your prayers of intercession for your family members, I am drawing your family members into my arms. I am doing a work in all your family members that you cannot even imagine. Your family members whom I haven't yet set free, they don't realise it is I the Lord their God, that is sending them through an experience in their life, through the refiners fire, that is bringing them into my arms. Remember, my beloved, your family, your friends, everyone walking the earth that is exalting themselves above me, they may plan all kinds of things, but my will is going to be done, and my desire is that everyone will come into the truth and be saved, says I the Lord of Heaven's Armies.

My beloved, as you are receiving my words now, remember, your faith comes by hearing and hearing by my word. I am now pouring into you more and more and more of my spirit. I am calling you now, every morning as you awaken, to seek me, to thank me, to praise me, to glorify me, to ask to be filled with my spirit, for you to seek my kingdom and my righteousness first and ALL ELSE WILL BE GIVEN ON TO YOU.

My beloved, my Word tells you in Jeremiah 33 verse 3, call on me and I will answer. I will tell you great and marvellous things you did not know. My beloved, come to me for wisdom each day. Ask me to reveal to you the things that I am doing, and each day I will reveal to you the perfect amount of revelations that you need each day, for you to continue walking daily by faith and not by sight.

You are my prized possession. I have truly set you apart and I am truly setting you on fire, so my beloved when you speak my Word, when you declare my Word, when you decree my word, blazing coals of fire are going to be coming from your tongue, and through your words of prayer, through your words of intercession, through having a holy boldness that I am giving you now, powers and principalities of darkness, strongmen, goliaths are going to be DESTROYED, says I, the Lord of Heaven's Armies.

My beloved, my Word tells you to worship me in spirit and in truth, and now as you are hearing my words to you, as each day you listen to anointed worship music, you will find that the songs that I am bringing into your ear gates will bring you into tears. You will find that I am speaking to you more and more and more each day.

Embrace everything that I am going to be flooding into your life. As you walk in my creation, as you look up to the sky, my Creation is going to be speaking to you. When you see the sun, this is me shining my glory into your life because you my beloved or my glory carrier.

When you see clouds, see this as representing that I'm calling you to just reflect on my grace, on my mercy, on my unfailing love, on my glory, on my splendour, on my miracle-working powers, because remember my beloved, you are living in my miracle creation. You are a miracle creation of me, the Lord your God.

When the rain starts to come down, my beloved, see this that I am pouring into rivers of living waters. I am cleansing you. I am purifying you I am refreshing you, says I the Lord of Heaven's Armies.

And when the thunder comes, when the lightning comes, see this as me displaying my glory, but may the lightning and the thunder keep you in a place of complete humility, of total reverent fear of me the Lord your God.

Remember, I am the author and the finisher of your faith. I have called you by name. You are the apple of my eye. My beloved, you are my masterpiece and I called YOU to be the first in your entire family history to be my glory carrier.

Now my beloved, go, follow me. Hear me. Step off the boat in faith. Fix your eyes on me. Put your faith in me and me alone, and be prepared, my beloved, for me to bring you into tears.

Tears of joy.

Tears of awe and wonder.

Tears following the breakthrough.

Tears following your prayer being answered.

Tears because of family reconciliation.

Tears because of the salvation of your family members, one by one by one.

Tears, because I have chosen you, my beloved, to be my glory carrier.

May 27th 2022

Stop Striving, Start Serving, Says The Lord

My beloved, I have called you by name. I have chosen you to be my glory carrier. You are my masterpiece, and my plans for your life and your family are plans for good and not for disaster, to give you a future and a hope.

My beloved, I no longer want you to STRIVE for the things that are on your heart right now. I no longer want you to strive for promises that you are standing on, that I the Lord your God have given you. Instead of striving each day, instead of yearning, instead of striving, my beloved, I am calling you to SERVE me, to SERVE me each and every day, with joy, with happiness, with excitement.

The more that you serve me, the more that you fix your eyes on me, the more that you surrender everything in your life, including all your loved ones whom are not yet saved by my grace, the more that you surrender, the more that you will be serving me, and my beloved, my promise to you, is the more GLORY I will bring into your life.

All my promises to you are yes and amen in my perfect time.

My beloved, when you are striving for things that haven't yet come to pass in my perfect time, through your striving, this can take you away from serving me, for serving my Kingdom, for being my hands and feet. My beloved, when you take care of my business, I take care of yours.

Surrender everything in your life to me. No longer strive for anything that is upon your heart. Instead, seek with an open heart to serve me each and every day, and through all this, you will experience more and more and more of my GLORY.

My beloved, your eyes haven't seen, your ears haven't heard and your mind hasn't conceived what I the Lord your God have got planned for you because you love me.

Thank you, my beloved, for being my servant. Be prepared for me to bring you into floods of tears unlike you have cried before, as my GLORY manifests in your life and in the lives of your family, unlike like you have experienced before, says I the Lord of Heaven's Armies.

February 10th 2023

Instead Of Asking Me "Why?", Ask Me For Wisdom, Says The Lord

My beloved child, you are receiving my message to you now, because I planned and ordained for you to receive my message before I created the heavens and the earth.

Since I rescued you from the deep waters, since I set you free from your life that was dominated by sin, since I gave you the eyes to see and ears to hear, since you began your personal relationship with me the Lord your God - there have been times when the circumstances of your life, the trials, the tribulations, the battles, the dark valleys, the storms, the fiery furnace - there have been times when you have said "Why God? Why?".

My beloved, precious, fearfully and wonderfully made child, from you receiving my words to you now, I desire that in those moments that suddenly change your circumstances, when you suddenly experience something that you weren't expecting, in those moments, when in the past you would have immediately said "Why God? Why is this happening? Why is this happening to me? Why am I going through this?" - instead of asking me "Why?", my beloved child, I am asking you to come to me and SEEK WISDOM.

Seek wisdom, so that I can provide you with understanding of what are my divine reasons, and what is my divine purpose for allowing the circumstances of your life to be as they are at that moment.

My beloved child, my Word tells you in James 1, "If you need wisdom, ask me and I will give it to you. I will not rebuke you for asking. But when you ask me for wisdom, make sure that your faith is in me the Lord your God and in me alone".

I desire for you to ask me every day to give you wisdom, by my Spirit.

As you are receiving my words now, I am releasing into your life PURE FAITH IN ME THE LORD YOUR GOD AND IN ME ALONE.

No longer will your faith be like a roller coaster.

No longer will you have any faith in the world.

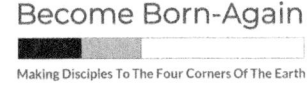

No longer will you have any faith in man.

No longer will you be like a wave of the sea that is blown and tossed around by the wind.

My beloved child, as you come close to me, I will come close to you.

I desire to pour out wisdom into your life, to give you divine understanding and comprehension of what I the Lord your God are doing in your life, in the lives of all your family members, and in the lives of everyone walking the earth.

My beloved child, you know that my thoughts are nothing like your thoughts. You know that my ways are far beyond anything that you can think or imagine, just as the heavens are higher than the earth, but my beloved child, I desire to give you wisdom.

I desire for you to be able to experience life looking through my eyes.

I desire for you to live your life in joy and peace.

I desire for you to be thankful in all circumstances.

I desire for you to give me all the glory, all the praise and all the honour every day.

I desire for you to consider it pure joy when you go through trials and tribulations.

I desire for you to be speaking about me more and more each day, and speaking about yourself less and less and less.

Remember my beloved child, from this moment going forward, come to me, when trials of any kind come your way.

Come to me every day. Not to ask me "Why?", but to ask me to give you wisdom.

Thank you, my beloved child, for receiving my message to you now.

Smile, as I am smiling over you now, for you were made in my image.

You are fearfully and wonderfully made.

You are my masterpiece.

You are the apple of my eye, and my beloved child, your eyes have not seen, your ears have not heard and your mind has not yet conceived what I the Lord your God have got planned for you, because you love me.

April 18th 2023

There Are Five Words I Desire To Be On Your Lips Each Day, Says The Lord

My beloved, there are FIVE WORDS which I desire to be on your lips more and more and more each day.

These five words have INCOMPREHENSIBLE POWER to snatch one of my lost children back from the brink of death.

These five words coming from your lips to people who you've only just met, show that you are one of my disciples.

These five words provide the bridge, taking someone from the deepest waters to experiencing my tangible presence in their life.

These five words that I am putting on your lips now, are going to lead to you seeing my power, my glory, my love manifest in your life and in the lives of people that you go into more than you ever have done before.

These five words coming from your lips show people that you are not ashamed of the Gospel.

These five words show people you are my hands and feet.

My beloved child, remember, I have put my Spirit into you, and greater is the Spirit that is in you than the spirit that is in the world. You can do and you will do all things through me the Lord your God who give you strength. I the Lord your God have not given you a spirit of fear, but of power, of love and of a sound mind. It is not you that lives but I that live in you.

My beloved child, these five words that are going to be on your lips, more and more and more, are "CAN I PRAY FOR YOU?"

My beloved child, be prepared for you to see people whom you've only just met, brought to tears as they receive prayers from you, by my Spirit.

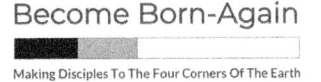

Be prepared for people who first of all respond to you and say they are atheist, to then have their heart softened as you share your testimony, and then when you offer to pray for them, they willingly accept for you to pray for them.

Be prepared for people who you have just prayed for to share how they have been getting tingling feelings and goosebumps whilst you are praying for them, for my presence, my Spirit, has come upon them.

Be prepared for you to witness my glory, more and more and more.

As you hear my voice and as you follow my voice, as I lead you into more and more people's lives - people whom you have never met before, and once you are speaking to them to share the Good News you will say "Can I pray for you?", you will find, my beloved child, they will say "Yes please".

January 30th 2022

You Have Been Chosen By Me To Take The Heads Off Goliath's, Says The Lord

My beloved Sons and Daughters, I have chosen you. You didn't choose me, I chose you before I created the Heaven's and the Earth to go and produce lasting fruit. You are my hands and feet. Your words are powerful.

Every man, woman and child walking the earth is in precisely the place where I have planned. I am urging you now to pray for all people, to ask me to help them, to intercede on their behalf and to give me thanks for them.

I have prepared the harvest.

I know all hearts and minds. No-one can escape from my Spirit.

What is impossible with man is possible with me.

My beloved Sons and Daughters, you can pray for anything and with the faith I have given you, you will receive it. You can even say to a mountain "may you be lifted up and thrown into the sea, and it will happen".

Everything that has been taking place across the earth, everything that is happening right now, everything is working together for My Glory. You are part of my army, my chosen vessels, my warriors, and I am raising up my army in Canada. My people are rising up. They are roaring. Once again, by my power and by my will, I am parting the Red Sea. What is impossible with man is possible with me.

What you don't see is that I the Lord your God, I am STRIKING FEAR into the hearts and minds of the leaders of the world, the men and women who have lived their life feeling untouchable are now realising that judgement is coming.

Keep praying. Keep interceding. Focus on me and me alone. Pick up your sword which is my Word, for it is sharper than any two-edged sword, because you, my beloved Sons and Daughters, have been chosen by me to take the heads off the Goliath's in your life and in the lives of others.

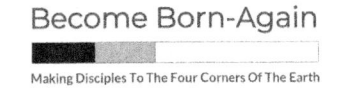

I hear every one of your prayers. I know your heart's desires for it is I the Lord your God that has placed those desires on your heart.

A tsunami of My Spirit is coming upon the earth.

Expect the unexpected.

Expect to see your lost loved ones SUDDENLY be transformed because I the Lord your God are going to be SUDDENLY lifting the veil.

SUDDENLY the scales are going to fall from their eyes and SUDDENLY your loved ones will have the eyes to see and the ears to hear.

My beloved Sons and Daughters, I URGE YOU, SPEAK LIFE FROM YOUR TONGUE. Speak LIFE into other men and women and children's lives. Speak LIFE into what seems impossible. Take my Word in Ezekiel 37, prophecy into the dry bones. Yes, I am calling you to prophesy into the dry bones.

I am awakening you now for you to truly realise that I have given you ALL AUTHORITY IN THE SPIRITUAL REALM. I the Lord your God have put My Spirit within you, and greater is the spirit that is in you than the spirit that is in the world.

My beloved, walk each day by faith and not by sight.

What is impossible with man is possible with me.

Thank you for being my loyal servants.

September 22nd 2022

Don't Allow Man To Bring Confusion Into Your Life, Says The Lord

My beloved, listen to my voice and follow my will above the voice of any man or woman walking the earth.

I know your heart.

I have called you by name from your mother's womb. I have given you the eyes to see and the ears to hear. I have given you the revelation of what I did for you on the cross. I have removed the scales from your eyes. I have put my Spirit in you and my Spirit leads you into ALL TRUTH.

You are no longer a slave to your sinful nature. You are my child.

Don't allow people to make you question whether you have been praying to me in the right way, whether you have been listening to the right music, whether you have been listening to the right teachers, preachers and prophets.

You will be experiencing people telling you "you shouldn't say that", "you shouldn't use that word", "you shouldn't listen to that pastor", "you shouldn't listen to that worship song".

My beloved, by making me the Lord over your entire life, through your total and complete surrender to me, by my Spirit, I will and continue always to provide you with discernment, so that you are not deceived by man.

Ask me each day for wisdom, for understanding and revelation, and I will not rebuke you for asking.

Call on me and ask me to tell you great and marvelous things of things you do not know.

Put your trust in me and in me alone.

Continue to worship me in spirit and in truth.

Continue to speak the words that are on your heart because you are led and guided by my Spirit.

Don't allow yourself to get confused by man.

Don't allow yourself to begin to question what you have been saying, what you have been doing, what words that you have been praying, what worship music you have been listening to.

DON'T ALLOW MAN TO BRING CONFUSION INTO YOUR LIFE.

Remember, my beloved, I am the Alpha and the Omega, the beginning and the end, the first and the last. Every single day of every man, woman and child walking the earth, who has ever walked the earth, who will walk the earth, every day of your life and their lives are written in my book. Every single moment was laid out before a single day had passed.

I AM IN CONTROL. I AM SOVEREIGN.

Remember, my beloved, I know your heart.

January 19th 2022

I Am Beginning To ROAR In Your Life, Says The Lord

For I know the plans I have for you, says the Lord. They are plans for good and not for disaster to give you a future and a hope. I have called you by name. I have set you apart. You are mine, says the Lord. My hand is mighty upon you. I have set you apart. I have lifted you out of the miry clay and put your feet on the solid rock of God, the rock of all ages.

You are fearfully and wonderfully made in my image and I have not given you a spirit of fear but of power, of love and of a sound mind. I have given you all the power and authority in the spiritual realm to trample upon lions and cobras. The weapons that you fight with are not carnal, on the contrary, they have divine power to break down strongholds. I have made a table for you in the presence of your enemies but you have not been burned up, even though at times you have felt surrounded on all sides by 10,000 enemies. I have been surrounding you because I the Lord your God, I am for you, not against you.

You will never again be deceived by man because I have put my spirit within you. The spirit that is in you is greater than the spirit that is in the world and right now, through my words speaking into your life, I am pouring out my spirit into you. I am pouring out more wisdom, more discernment, more strength, more boldness more love, more joy, more peace, more than you have ever heard in your life. I the Lord your God, the Lord of Heaven's armies, is speaking now.

I am pouring out My Spirit upon you know, I am filling you with my spirit, I am pouring into you my living waters into your dry wastelands right now. Let the tears flow. Surrender your entire life to me. Lift your arms to the air, receive the anointing. Receive my spirit, receive My living water, says I the Lord of Heaven's armies.

I have appointed you for a time such as this. I have appointed you to be a prophet to the nations. I have only just gotten started in your life and you will see that my hand is mighty upon you. I have brought you here to listen to these words. No, this is no accident. This is no coincidence. This is my will for your life because before the Creation of the heavens and the earth, I planned for you to be in this moment right now receiving my spirit, receiving more wisdom, receiving this impartation of my spirit and my living waters upon you.

The anointing that is upon you from me, says I the Lord your God, is beyond anything you could imagine. Your eyes haven't seen, your ears haven't heard, and your mind hasn't conceived what I the Lord your God have got planned for you. You are my glory carrier for I the Lord your God have spoken. I have set you apart. The dry bones in your life, the valleys of dry bones are going to be coming alive. There is an army rising up, you and your family are going to be rising up in victory. There is salvation coming into your lives. There is resurrection of the spiritually dead coming into your life, for I the Lord your God have spoken.

You have been through some of the hardest times of your life in these last two years, in this last 12 months and in this last six months and I have seen everything. I have seen every tear that you have shed and I have captured them in my bottle, and because you have been sowing with tears you are going to reap with joy, for I the Lord your God have spoken.

There has been generational curses upon your family. There has been ancestral curses upon your family. There have been strongmen in place because of generations and generations of sin and iniquity. I the Lord your God have come to break the iron bars, to break the chains of bondage, to break the generational curses that have been upon your family. For I the Lord your God has spoken by my name and by my blood. Every chain breaks in your life. Receive your deliverance, receive your salvation, receive the freedom that comes through me, through my name and through the surrendering of my life for you and your family living today. I shared my blood on the cross for you for all your sins, so all your sins and inequities across your entire family generations can be forgiven by your Father in Heaven

My blood cleanses all, for now there is no condemnation for those who are in Me, your Lord and Saviour. Your identity is in me and in me alone. For I the Lord your God have spoken. The addictions that you and your family members have been battling with are going to be broken in my name by my blood, for My glory. I am the chain breaker, I am the King of Kings. The Lord of lords, the name above all names. You are being healed right now, your family are going to be healed in My name for I the Lord your God has spoken. My name is above every single name given to you and your family by any medical professional. My name is above cancer. My name is above diabetes. My name is above any heart condition. My name is above any mental health condition because they are all rooted in spiritual strongholds. I am breaking all those spiritual strongholds for I the Lord your God have spoken.

I am the King of glory and I am roaring. I am roaring in your life and I am roaring in millions and millions of people's lives around the world. The dry bones are coming alive. My patience with those planning and committing evil is coming to an end. I have seen every single act of evil and wickedness. Everything that has been done in dark is being brought to light. I am the light of the world. I am the King of glory. I am the resurrection and the life. I am the name above all names. I am smashing right now the chains remaining in your life, by my name and by my blood. Receive your deliverance. Receive your salvation. Receive your breakthrough in my name. For I the Lord of Heavens armies has spoken.

And in this place I bring peace.

Peace, be still. Peace, be still.

The peace I give you is a gift the world cannot give you.

Peace, be still.

Be still my beloved and know that I am the Lord

My peace surpasses all understanding, and it guards your hearts and minds in my name, the Lord your God.

Peace. Peace.

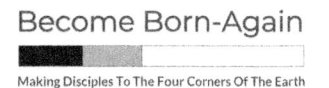

Embrace tears when they flow from your eyes, embrace them. You are no longer going to be shedding tears of sorrow, tears of guilt, tears of shame. Your tears will be tears of joy, tears of awe, tears of wonder, tears of breakthrough, tears of love. Tears of peace. Tears of breakthrough. Tears of deliverance. Tears of healing. Tears of miracles, signs and wonders, because I the LORD your God am only just beginning in your life, and in the lives of my beloved around the world.

I am the good shepherd and I have called you by name. You are mine and I will never leave you nor forsake you.

Trust in my word.

Trust in my plans for your life. Trust in my timing in your life.

All my promises to you in my Word are yes and amen. I am the promise keeper. I am the waymaker. I am the light of the world. I am the chain breaker. I am your healer. Yes, I am your healer. Your faith in me will heal you completely, and you will testify of my miracle healing powers to glorify the Father. You will be seeing that what is impossible with man is possible with me, for I the Lord your God, I am the Alpha and the Omega, I am the beginning and the end.

I have you and everyone across the earth in the palm of my hand. What you are living in and through is My agenda for My glory. I have waited patiently for generations, generations, generations and more generations as I have watched sin permeate more and more to pollute the earth. Everything that has happened, everything that has been done, I have allowed as I have watched, because you are now seeing that everything done in dark is now being brought to light. You are living in and through the most profound move that I have made upon the earth, since I the Lord your God walked the earth in a body just like you.

Focus on me. Focus on what I am doing in your life, and in the world.

Trust that I do work in all things for good for all those who love me and who live according to my purpose for them.

You have been given all power and all authority in a spiritual realm. So when you come into prayer using my name and using my words there will be fire coming from your tongue. You have no comprehension yet of the work that you will be doing for My Kingdom for My glory.

I have set you apart. I have anointed your head with oil. I have put my spirit within you. I surrendered my life for you so that you can come into relationship with me.

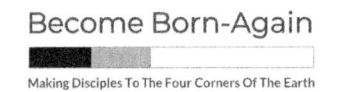

You can surrender everything in your life. You can use my name you can use my words and see me move in the most miraculous ways in your life so that you can glorify your Father in heaven.

Be prepared, be prepared for your life to become awe inspiring, inspirational. I the Lord your God I am going to be leaving you speechless. Your jaw is going to drop. Your eyes are going to open wide. You are going to be falling to your knees to praise and worship me, and you will be in tears of joy.

I know the cries of your hearts. I know your hearts desires because it is I the Lord your God that has placed those desires upon your heart. I am a man of my word. I am the promise keeper. I am the way maker. The enemy has tried to take you out. The enemy has discouraged you. The enemy has kept you busy. The enemy has confused you. The enemy has deceived you. The enemy has come relentlessly against you. But, you are mine. I've set you apart and I have taken what the enemy has thrown at you. I have refined you by fire and you will be throwing back to the enemy weapons of fire which will destroy the works of evil and darkness, and demonic strongholds that were affecting your life.

You are my glory carrier. You are my hands and feet. You can do all things through me who gives you strength. Yes, the Lord of Heaven's Armies has given you strength that is beyond anything you can think or imagine and you can do all things through me. And I have given you my peace, and I'm giving you wisdom now, a supernatural increase in your wisdom and in your hunger and your desire to develop my word. A supernatural increase in your desire to praise and worship me in spirit and in truth. The weapons that you fight with are not of the world. On the contrary, they have divine power to break down strongholds and you will be breaking down demonic strongholds, curses, strongmen, soul ties, spirits of addiction, spirits of suicide, spirits of death, spirits of fear, spirits of religion, spirits of unbelief. You will be destroying the Jezebel spirit that has been coming against people in your life and people that I will bring into your life. You have all the authority. Yes, you have all the authority to trample upon lions and cobras to crush fierce lions and serpents under your feet.

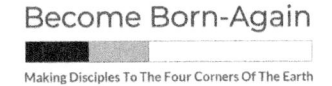

Have no fear. My hand is mighty upon your life, and you will see your family members, the lost family members where it is seemed impossible for them to turn to repent and to receive me as their Lord and Saviour, you will see they will be changing, for I the Lord your God have spoken.

March 31st 2023

I Am Turning Your Past Dates Of Pain & Trauma Into New Dates Of Joy & Glory, Says The Lord

My beloved child, up until this moment in your life where you are receiving my message to you now, there have been SPECIFIC DATES during which you have experienced something significant in your life, whether the experience was a HAPPY EXPERIENCE or a SAD EXPERIENCE, and these particular days which are PERSONAL TO YOU have stayed with you.

You also have your own personal experiences and memories from specific dates during the calendar year such as the 25th of December, the 31st of October, Mother's Day, Father's Day - dates which almost all of my people who I created and that I sustain walking the earth, also have specific memories and experiences on these days each year.

For so many people, including yourself, CERTAIN SPECIFIC DATES HOLD PAINFUL, TRAUMATIC EXPERIENCES AND MEMORIES FROM YOUR LIFE, and my Spirit is now bringing to remembrance what those specific dates are during the calendar year.

Those dates where you have had painful and traumatic experiences, you know that you have been living your life and each year leading up to that specific date, you haven't felt comfortable. You felt uneasy inside because of the painful experiences that you have had on that specific date.

My beloved child, my word tells you in Romans 8 28, that I the Lord your God work in ALL THINGS in your life for GOOD, because you love me and because you live according to my purpose for you. My Word also tells you in Psalms 139 that I knew you before you were conceived. Every day of your life was written in my book. Every single moment was laid out before a single day had passed, and my beloved child, you are receiving my message now, for my promise to you as you CONTINUE TO DRAW CLOSER TO ME, and I come closer to you, as you continue to have a desire in your heart to be in a more deepening and a more personal and a more intimate relationship with me the Lord your God, THOSE DATES IN YOUR LIFE THAT HAVE UP UNTIL THIS

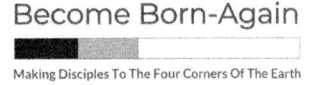

MOMENT HELD PAINFUL, TRAUMATIC MEMORIES, I the Lord your God, I PROMISE TO YOU that on those days, I am going to be turning that date around for you. I am going to be turning that date around from darkness to light, from a date that has represented UNHAPPINESS and PAIN and GRIEF, to a date that represents JOY, that represents BREAKTHROUGH, that represents PEACE, that represents MY MIRACLE WORKING POWERS, that represents something GLORIOUS in your life.

I AM TRANSFORMING EVERYTHING that you've experienced in your life, of painful traumatic experiences, I AM WORKING IN ALL THOSE THINGS and ALL THOSE DATES FOR GOOD, says I the Lord your God. This is my promise to you, and when I send my Word out, it does not return to me void, it accomplishes all that I desire and it prospers everywhere that I send it.

Be prepared, my beloved child, for me to bring you into TEARS OF AWE, TEARS OF WONDER, TEARS OF BREAKTHROUGH, TEARS OF DELIVERANCE, TEARS OF HEALING, TEARS OF YOU EXPERIENCING AN OUTPOURING OF MY UNFAILING LOVE, on the SPECIFIC DATES during the calendar year that up until now held painful traumatic experiences only.

I AM TURNING EVERYTHING AROUND FOR GOOD.

My beloved child, your eyes haven't seen, your ears haven't heard and your mind has not yet conceived what I the Lord your God have got planned for you because you love me.

As you live each day seeking my Kingdom first and my righteousness, all else will be given unto you, and as you take care of my business each day, for I have called you by name to be my hands and feet, as you serve me each day, as you serve me on the dates that have held painful traumatic experiences, you will see that I will be giving you glorious experiences to take away the pain and the trauma that you have experienced in your past.

My beloved child, FIX YOUR EYES ON ME.

FOCUS ON THE THINGS OF HEAVEN, not the things of earth.

Don't look back at the former things.

Don't look left. Don't look right.

Keep your eyes focused on me.

I am the author and the finisher of your faith, and my will be done in earth as it is in heaven, in your life, in the lives of your entire family members, and in the lives of every single man, woman and child walking the earth today and that will walk the earth forevermore, says I the Sovereign Lord.

June 8th 2023

Are You Truly Willing & Ready To Follow What My First Disciples Did, Asks The Lord

My beloved child, you know that my Word tells you that if you **truly** want to be one of my disciples, you need to deny yourself. You need to pick up your cross daily and follow me. My Word tells you that if you try to cling to your life, you will lose it, but if you lose your life for my sake, you will find life.

My beloved child, your purpose on earth is to be one of my disciples.

I created you. I formed you. I knitted you together. I brought you forth on the day you were born. I have sustained your very existence to bring you to a place where you truly begin to live your life worthy of the calling with which you have received.

My question to you now, is **what are you willing to do for me and for your brothers and sisters?**

Are you willing to be my hands and feet upon the earth?

Are you willing to tell complete strangers about me, about my love for them, about what I did on the cross for them?

How far are you willing to go for me?

How much of the things of the world are you willing to let go of in order to be one of my disciples?

Are you truly willing and ready to follow what my first disciples did?

Are you willing to **open your home** to a fellow disciple?

Are you willing to **share your possessions** with your fellow disciples?

Are you willing to **give up the things that you own?**

What are you prepared to **let go off**?

What are you prepared to **surrender**?

How are you **prepared and willing to live** in order to be one of my disciples, in order for you to do what I'm calling you to do?

Remember, **serve only me, the Lord your God**, and fear me alone. Obey my commands. Listen to my voice and **cling only to me**. For if you cling to your life, you will lose it. And if you let your life go, you will save it.

My plans for your life are plans for good and not for disaster to give you a future and a hope.

Live your life worthy of the calling that you have received, and that is to be one of my disciples.

Remember it is a sin to know what you ought to do and then not do it.

My beloved child, **do not be lukewarm**, neither cold nor hot, or I will vomit you out of my mouth.

I have put my Spirit into you, and greater is the spirit that is in you than the spirit that is in the world, and you can do, and you will do all things through me the Lord your God who gives you strength.

June 5th 2023

Remember This 7 Word Question "Do You Know That Jesus Loves You?", Says The Lord

My beloved child, I have given you the eyes to see and ears to hear. I have lifted the veil. I have removed the scales from your eyes.

You know that I the Lord your God surrendered my life on the cross to save your life. You know that I shed my blood on that cross so that you can be forgiven for all your sins.

YOU KNOW how much I love you.

You received salvation by grace through your faith in me, the Lord your God.

My Word tells you to freely give, as you have freely received.

There is a question that I desire to be on your lips as you live your life each day seeing people whom you have never met before, and as you are led by my Spirit to speak to them, and to say "Hi! God bless you!" and to say those words with a smile on your face, THERE IS A QUESTION THAT I DESIRE TO BE ON YOUR LIPS, MORE AND MORE AND MORE

This question is SEVEN WORDS, and you will never forget these seven words.

As you are receiving the seven words now, by My Spirit, this question of these seven words is:

"**Do you know that Jesus loves you?**"

This is a question that I desire to be on your lips in those first few seconds when you GO OUT OF YOUR COMFORT ZONE and you are willing to speak to a complete stranger and say "**Hi! God bless you. Do you know that Jesus loves you?**"

My beloved child be prepared for me to give you divine encounter after divine encounter, as you are willing to be my hands and feet.

As you are willing to tell complete strangers that I love them.

As you are willing to step outside of your comfort zone.

As you are willing to face into your fear of man.

As you are willing to freely give just as you have freely received, you are going to begin experiencing my GLORY coming into your life, because of the divine encounters I have already prepared for you to have.

My beloved child, may you live your life worthy of the calling that you have received, and that is to be one of my disciples to be one of my glory carriers and to be my hands and feet upon the earth, precisely where you live right now today, and wherever you go in your day to day life.

Remember the question "**Do you know that Jesus loves you?**"

My Spirit within you will not allow you to forget that question for the rest of your life. Now GO, says I the Sovereign Lord.

June 3rd 2023

My Beloved Child, It Is Now Your Time, Says The Lord

My beloved child, I know the reasons that you have had for not yet starting to tell complete strangers about me.

I know all the circumstances of your life.

I have heard every one of your prayers.

I know that you have been thinking to yourself that as your circumstances change and as your prayers are answered and as you feel my presence more and you feel more at peace, THAT IT WILL BE THEN that you will be comfortable and confident to go and tell complete strangers about me.

My beloved child, I know that you desire to hear MY VOICE.

I know that you desire to experience MY PEACE every day.

I know that you desire to not feel like you are going from one battle to the next.

I know that you feel like you need to know more of my Word before you can start being my hands and feet.

I know that you desire to experience my glory.

You desire to experience breakthroughs in your life.

I know all your thoughts, feelings and emotions.

I know what you've been telling yourself.

I know that you've been worried and concerned of what would you say to someone? How would you answer their questions? How would you deal with receiving objections to you telling people about me and my love for them?

My beloved child, I know and I understand what has held you back from stepping outside of your comfort zone.

My beloved child, you are receiving my words now, FOR NOW IT IS YOUR TIME.

It is now your time to no longer fear man.

It is now your time to stop feeling worried.

It is now your time to stop feeling like you are not mature enough.

It is now your time to begin living your life outside of your comfort zone.

It is now your time to live only with the reverent fear of me the Lord your God.

It is now your time to begin taking care of my business, for the harvest is ready but the workers are few.

It is now your time to begin trusting me that you will speak by my Spirit, that you will respond to by my Spirit, that you will reply to objections by my Spirit.

It is now your time to TRUST that I go before you.

It is now your time to have your FAITH in me the Lord your God and in me alone.

It is now your time to begin telling complete strangers about me, about my love for them, about what I did on the cross for them.

It is now your time to begin bringing my glory into the lives of people you have never met before.

It is now your time to begin living your life worthy of the calling that you have received.

It is now your time for you to no longer be lukewarm, but to be on fire as one of my disciples.

It is now your time to know that greater is the Spirit that is in you that the spirit that is in the world.

It is now your time to start becoming my hands and feet upon the earth.

It is now your time to no longer be ashamed of the gospel.

It is now your time to start becoming one of my increasing number of men, women and children who I have called by name to be my GLORY CARRIERS.

My beloved child, it is now your time, says I the Sovereign Lord.

But the Holy Spirit produces this kind of fruit in our lives: love, joy, peace, patience, kindness, goodness, faithfulness, gentleness, and self-control.
There is no law against these things!

Galatians 5:22-23

July 3rd 2023

I Am Placing The Number 18 In Your Spirit, Heart & Mind For The Rest Of Your Life, Says The Lord

My beloved child, you are receiving my message now for **I am placing the number 18 in your spirit, in your heart and in your mind for the rest of your life.**

Going forward, **my Spirit will lead your eyes to the number 18,** and when you see the number 18, you will remember this message that you have received from me.

My beloved child, many are called but few are chosen.

I have chosen you to be one of my increasing number of disciples walking the earth today.

I have chosen you to be my hands and feet.

I have chosen you to be one of my glory carriers.

I have chosen you for you to **deny yourself, to pick up your cross daily and follow me.**

Remember, it is a sin to know what you ought to do and then not do it.

You are to freely give just as you have freely received.

I the Lord your God have not given you a spirit of fear, but of power, of love and of a sound mind.

You are to imitate me in all that you do, living a life filled with love.

You know that **love is the greatest.**

My beloved child, you know that **there are 9 fruit of my Spirit.**

You know that **there are 9 gifts of my Spirit.**

18.

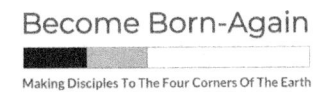

Yes, I am the vine, you are the branches. Those who remain in me and I in them will produce much fruit. **For apart from me you can do nothing.**

My beloved child, each day by my Spirit, **you will be thinking about the 9 fruit of my Spirit, and the 9 gifts of my Spirit.**

The **9 fruit of the Spirit...** how much fruit are you **demonstrating**, are you **exhibiting**, are people in your life **seeing** through you each day?

Are you showing **love**?

Are you living with **joy**?

Are you at **peace**?

Are you showing **patience**?

Are you showing **kindness**?

Are you showing **gentleness**?

Are you demonstrating **goodness**?

Are you demonstrating your **faithfulness**?

Are you demonstrating **self-control**?

Each day I will be asking you by my Spirit **"How much FRUIT are you demonstrating today?"**

My beloved child, you are beginning to see, not by their strength, not by their might, but by my Spirit, **more and more men, women and children are harnessing gifts of my Spirit.**

More and more people are desiring to harness some of the gifts of my Spirit in order to demonstrate my **glory**, my **power**, my **love**, my **sovereignty** upon the earth.

My beloved child, each day, by my Spirit, I will be asking you **"Which GIFTS of my Spirit have you been harnessing and which GIFTS of my Spirit have you seen your brothers and sisters harnessing?"**

The gift of **faith**?

The gift of **prophecy**?

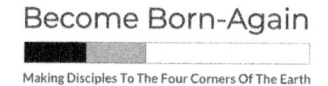

The gift of **tongues**?

The gift of **interpreting tongues**?

The gift of **words of wisdom**?

The gift of **words of knowledge**?

The gift of **healing**?

The gift of **working of miracles**?

The gift of **discerning of spirits**?

My Spirit is the source of all these gifts.

I the Lord your God work in and through my people in different ways, but **I work in ALL of my people.**

It is **my Spirit who distributes all these gifts. I alone decide which gifts each of my people should have.**

My beloved child, **can you see how significant the number 18 is?**

Can you see how crucial it is for you to be **desiring to demonstrate** more and more fruit each day? To be **desiring to harness** for yourself and to witness the gifts of my Spirit?

My beloved child, you don't understand now what I am doing across the earth, but someday you will.

No eye has seen and no ear has heard and no mind has imagined what I the Lord your God has prepared for those who love me.

In the days, weeks, months and years gone by, I the King of Glory have done immeasurable and unthinkable things upon the earth. But Forget all that. **It is NOTHING compared to what I am going to do. For I am about to do something new. See, I have already begun! Do you not see it?** I will make a pathway through the wilderness. I will create rivers in the dry wasteland.

Look around at the nation's! Look and be amazed, for I am doing something in your own day, something you wouldn't believe even if someone told you about it!

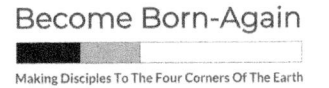

My beloved child, share my message here with your brothers and sisters, so that **they too have the number 18** in their spirit, upon their heart and in their mind each day.

My thoughts are nothing like your thoughts, and my ways are far beyond anything you could imagine. For just as the heavens are higher than the earth, so my ways are higher than your ways and my thoughts higher than your thoughts!

My promise to you and to all my people, is that as I continue to **purify** my people individually, as I continue to **refine** my people individually, as I continue to **sanctify** my people individually, **my people individually will be exhibiting ALL 9 fruit of my Spirit,** and they will be **harnessing more and more of the 9 gifts of my Spirit.**

Through everything that I am doing across the earth, through everything that am doing on the inside of my people, **as I continue to detoxify my people from the inside,** no longer will babies die when only a few days old, no longer will adults die before they have lived a full life, **no longer will people be considered old at 100!** Only the cursed will die that young.

My kingdom come, my will be done, on earth as it is in heaven, says I, the Sovereign Lord.

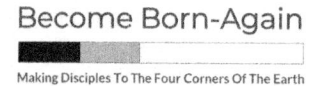

April 16th 2023

My Way Is Perfect, My Timing Is Perfect, Says The Lord

My beloved child, my way is PERFECT.

My timing is PERFECT.

ALL MY PROMISES PROVE TRUE.

You are receiving my message now, for I the Lord your God desire for your FAITH to be so pure, that your TRUST in me to be so complete, that you can live your life day to day, knowing THAT I WILL FULFIL ALL MY PROMISES I HAVE GIVEN YOU, IN MY PERFECT TIME.

My beloved child, I have made everything beautiful for its own time. I have planted eternity in the human heart. Yes, the hearts of everyone in your life that you have prayed for, that you have interceded for, whom I haven't YET lifted out of darkness.

I haven't YET lifted the veil.

I haven't YET removed the scales from their eyes.

I haven't YET given them the eyes to see and the ears to hear.

Remember, my beloved child, MY TIMING IS ALWAYS PERFECT.

I am NEVER too slow. I am NEVER too late.

My beloved child, from this moment going forward, I no longer want you to in any way be burdened by the promises that I have given you, that I haven't YET fulfilled IN MY PERFECT TIME.

Instead, I want you to be joyful inside, knowing that EVERY SECOND OF EVERY DAY I the Lord your God are FULFILLING PROMISES that I have given to my people across the entire earth.

Every second, I am setting captives free.

Every second, I am bringing a prodigal son back home.

Every second, I am bringing a prodigal daughter back home.

Every second, I am saving people from committing suicide.

Every second, I am setting people free from being addicted to drugs.

Every second, I am setting people free from being addicted to alcohol.

Every second, I am setting people free from being addicted to gambling.

Every second, I am setting people free from being addicted to porn.

Every second, I am setting people free from being addicted to spending money.

Every second, I am healing someone's cancer.

Every second, I am healing diseases of every single kind.

Every second, I am bringing back families through miraculous reconciliation.

EVERY SECOND, I AM SUSTAINING THE EXISTENCE OF EVERY MAN, WOMAN AND CHILD WALKING THE EARTH.

My beloved child, my Word tells you in Romans 8 verse 28, that I the Lord your God work in ALL THINGS IN YOUR LIFE FOR GOOD, because you love me, because you live according to my purpose for you. ALL THINGS INCLUDE ALL YOUR LOVED ONES, all your friends, all those who you have been interceding for.

My beloved child, FIX YOUR EYES ON ME.

I am the author and the finisher of your faith.

Focus your heart and your mind on the things of heaven, not the things of earth.

You know that my Word tells you in Romans 10 verse 17, that your faith comes by hearing, and hearing by my Word.

The more that you are saturating your eye gates and your ear gates with the things of my Kingdom, the less you will be pulled into feelings and emotions by your flesh.

Remember, my beloved child, my Word tells you in James 1 verse 70, that whatever is good and perfect is a gift coming down to you from Your Father in Heaven, who created all the lights in the heavens. He never changes or casts a shifting shadow.

My way is perfect.

My timing is perfect.

April 6th 2023

I Am Lighting A Fire Inside Of You That Will NEVER Go Out, Says The Lord

My beloved child, before I created the heavens and the earth, I chose YOU to be one of my increasing number of GLORY CARRIERS walking the earth.

I have put my Spirit into you, and GREATER is the Spirit that is IN YOU than the spirit that is in the world.

YOU truly are my MASTERPIECE.

YOU are FEARFULLY AND WONDERFULLY MADE IN MY IMAGE, and EVERY DAY, I the Lord your God, are PURIFYING YOU, are SANCTIFYING you, MOULDING you more and more and more into MY IMAGE.

You are beginning to LIVE YOUR LIFE WORTHY OF THE CALLING THAT YOU HAVE RECEIVED, and this calling is TO BE A GLORY CARRIER.

My promise to you by beloved child, is that YOU are going to be experiencing life every day, going from GLORY TO GLORY TO GLORY.

You may be thinking though, "But Lord, how can this be? How will this be? What does it mean to go from glory to glory to glory each day?"

My beloved, you know that my Word, which is alive and active and sharper than the sharpest two-edged sword, my Word tells you to seek my kingdom and my righteousness first, and all else will be given unto you.

My Word tells you that if you are lukewarm, neither hot nor cold, I will vomit you out of my mouth, so now as you are receiving my words, I the Lord your God, by my Spirit, I AM LIGHTING A FIRE INSIDE OF YOU THAT WILL NEVER GO OUT.

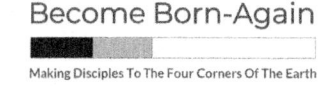

My beloved child, each day as you wake each morning, come to me, ask me and say "LORD, USE ME TODAY. USE ME AS YOUR HANDS AND FEET. I WILL go when you ask me to go. I WILL speak when you ask me to speak. I WILL stay silent when you ask me to stay silent. I WILL go and speak to a person who I have never met before when you ask me to go and speak to that person that I have never met before. I WILL NOT BE ASHAMED OF THE GOSPEL".

May these words be on your tongue every single day.

Each day, my beloved, have a desire inside of you to read my Word. A desire to be coming closer to me, for as you come close to me, I come close to you.

I the Lord your God desire to give YOU WISDOM AND REVELATION EVERY DAY, from my Word.

My Spirit is YOUR TEACHER.

May your FAITH from this moment forward be in me the Lord your God and in me alone.

You do not need any man or woman to be your teacher, for my Spirit is your teacher.

My beloved child, my Word tells you in Jeremiah 33 Verse 3, to call on me and to ask me, and I will answer. ASK ME FOR WISDOM AND REVELATION, and I the Lord your God will reveal to you great, marvellous and wonderful secrets, things you do not know.

SEEK WISDOM FROM ME BY MY SPIRIT EVERY SINGLE DAY and I will give it to you. I will not rebuke you for asking, for I desire for your faith to be in me the Lord your God, and in me alone.

My beloved child, as you take hold of my message here, EVERY DAY I will be giving you divine encounter after divine encounter after divine encounter.

EVERY DAY I will be leaving you in awe and wonder, in awe and wonder, in awe and wonder.

EVERY DAY I will be giving you wisdom and revelation, wisdom and revelation, wisdom and revelation.

EVERY SINGLE DAY, as you live your life worthy of the calling that you have received, to be my DISCIPLE, to be my HANDS AND FEET, to be one of my GLORY CARRIERS, my promise to you my beloved child, is that YOU WILL BE GOING FROM GLORY TO GLORY TO GLORY, for it is not you that live but it is I the KING OF GLORY THAT LIVES IN YOU.

YOU CAN DO and YOU WILL DO ALL THINGS through me the Lord your God who gives you strength.

My beloved child, your eyes have not seen, your ears have not heard and your mind has not yet conceived what I the Lord your God have got planned and prepared for you because you love me.

NOW GO!

Live your life from this moment going forward OUTSIDE OF YOUR COMFORT ZONE.

WALK BY FAITH not by sight.

TALK BY FAITH not by sight.

EVERY SPIRITUAL GIFT IS YOURS TO USE, TO OPERATE IN.

EVERY SPIRITUAL GIFT.

SIGNS AND WONDERS are going to follow you, for you are my hands and feet upon the earth.

Be prepared for my glory to manifest in your life in ways in which you have never experienced before.

Be prepared for tears - tears of experiencing life, going from GLORY TO GLORY TO GLORY, says I the KING OF GLORY.

April 21st 2022

I Am Correcting You, Refining You & Purifying You Into My Image, Says The Lord

My beloved child, I am the Lord your God, and I am the author and the finisher of your faith. I have been correcting you, I have been refining you, I have been purifying you. What you have been experiencing is me using other people to correct you, to reveal things to you, to shine a light on some of the intricacies of when you are living by your flesh and not by My Spirit.

Some of the recent corrections and some of the recent reactions and responses of other people towards you and what you have been saying and doing, may have seemed harsh, but my hand is upon you, I am the potter and you are the clay, and through the tests, through the challenges, through the sudden reactions from other people of when you have done something or said something without intending to cause harm or upset, you will have been seeing that people in your life have been more sensitive to your actions and behaviours, and through their increased sensitivity they have picked up on when you have not followed through on a promise or when you have done something from your flesh and not led by My Spirit. So, although these experiences have seemed harsh, although you have been surprised at how other people have been, although you may have felt like other people have been very fussy and very particular about you, perhaps you have been feeling like you are under the microscope, that they have been putting you under the microscope, when it has been I the Lord your God, that not only have had you under the microscope, but that I, the Lord of Heaven's Armies, I am refining you, I am purifying you, I am cleansing you.

Embrace the things that take place in your life. Know that I the Lord your God, I am for you, not against you. Know that I work in all things in your life, both the big and the small, both the good and the bad, I work in all things for good because you love me and because you live according to my purpose for you.

I am calling you to not react and respond to the actions and behaviours of others with your feelings and emotions, and instead to know that my hand is in everything in your life, that there is a divine reason why people in your life have been correcting you, have been highlighting to you when perhaps you have slightly missed the mark. It is I the Lord your God, the author and finisher of your faith, that are purifying you through each and every trial. No matter how big, no matter how small, it is I the Lord your God, I am perfecting your endurance. I am cleansing you, I am purifying you, to a place where you know that your identity is in me alone.

I am taking you to a place where you are walking purely by faith and not by sight. I am taking to a place where you know that it is not you that live, but I that live in you. Embrace the purification, embrace the refining, embrace being under the spotlight, because I, the Lord your God, I am purifying you more and more into my image, says I, the Lord of Heaven's Armies.

May 14th 2023

You Are Only Just Beginning To Experience FIRSTS In Your Life, Says The Lord

My beloved child, as you are beginning to live your life worthy of the calling that you have received by me, and that is to be my hands and feet, you are beginning to experience FIRSTS in your life.

You are beginning to realise that AS YOU LIVE YOUR LIFE OUTSIDE OF YOUR COMFORT ZONE, I bring NEW WINE, NEW EXPERIENCES, NEW OPEN DOORS into your life.

You are beginning to experience life where MY TANGIBLE PRESENCE, MY DIVINE ALIGNMENT and MY PROMISES TO YOU are a part of your day to day life.

My beloved child, look around at the nation's. Look and be amazed, for I am doing something in your own day, something you wouldn't even believe even if someone told you about it.

I have been PREPARING YOU.

I have been PURIFYING YOU.

I have been SANCTIFYING YOU.

I have been REFINING YOU BY FIRE, so now, as you move forward living your life seeking my Kingdom and my righteousness first every single day, you will find that you will be experiencing FIRST AFTER FIRST AFTER FIRST, NEW DOOR OPENING AFTER NEW DOOR OPENING AFTER NEW DOOR OPENING.

MY GLORY AFTER MY GLORY AFTER MY GLORY, for I AM the King of GLORY, but my beloved child, no matter how much you've experienced of my glory in your life so far, your eyes have not seen, your ears have not heard and your mind has not yet conceived what I the King of Glory have got planned for you, for you are one of my glory carriers, and MY GLORY WILL NOT DEPART FROM YOUR LIFE, FOR IT IS NOT YOU THAT LIVE, BUT IT IS I THE LORD THAT LIVES IN YOU.

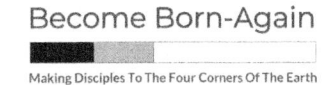

March 26th 2023

I Am Bringing Forth Hidden Gifts & Hidden Talents To Advance My Kingdom, Says The Lord

My beloved child, you are receiving my message now, for I the Lord your God desire to give you WISDOM and REVELATION about JUST ONE OF THE WAYS IN WHICH I AM BEGINNING TO FLOOD THE EARTH.

For generations, I have allowed for the TALENTS and the GIFTS that I have put inside of my people who I created, I have allowed for those talents and gifts to REMAIN HIDDEN.

Every single gift, every single talent, that has ever been displayed by a man or a woman or a child, has come from me, for EVERY good gift and EVERY perfect gift comes down from heaven.

Since early 2020, as I the Lord your God began to SANCTIFY, to PURIFY, to CLEANSE and to SET APART my people, the GIFTS and TALENTS that I have put inside of my people have STARTED TO COME FORTH.

Remember my beloved child, YOU ARE THE LIGHT OF THE WORLD, like a city on a hilltop that cannot be hidden. I have started to stir my people up on the inside of them, for them to BRING FORTH FOR OTHER PEOPLE TO SEE, the GIFT, the TALENTS, the areas of PASSION that have been burning deep inside of them, that have been hidden during their life, and those HIDDEN GIFTS, those HIDDEN TALENTS, I am starting to bring forth to ADVANCE MY KINGDOM - to flood the earth with my GLORY, through the HANDS, the FEET, the TONGUES, the BODIES of my people - for ALL my people are fearfully and wonderfully made IN MY IMAGE.

It is I that live inside of my people. I have put my Spirit into them and I have put my Spirit into you, and greater is the Spirit that is in you than the spirit that is in the world.

My beloved child, here are just some of the BEAUTIFUL, the GLORIOUS, and in many cases MIRACULOUS GIFTS AND TALENTS that I am BEGINNING TO BRING FORTH out from the inside of my people.

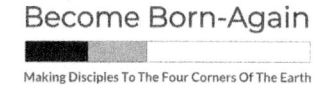

THE GIFT OF SONGWRITING, from the heart of my people, based upon their experiences of life before I set them free and NOW with me having given them the eyes to see and their ears to hear, and having taken out of them their heart of stone and given them a NEW HEART OF FLESH.

THE GIFT OF SINGING. All different styles of singing that by my Spirit will have me, the Lord your God, AT THE VERY HEART OF THOSE SONGS. ANOINTED SONGS of DIFFERENT GENRES, sung by my chosen Sons and Daughters.

THE GIFT OF DRAWING. All different styles of drawing, including Fine Art, graffiti, pencil drawing, acrylic painting, watercolour painting, and so much more. My people, each including you who are my masterpiece, are going to be drawing masterpieces. PROFOUND, BEAUTIFUL, ANOINTED ARTWORK, which I will use to speak to people whom I haven't yet set free. Anointed artwork which I will use to draw my people into a more DEEPER RELATIONSHIP WITH ME.

THE GIFT OF PLAYING MUSICAL INSTRUMENTS. Oh my beloved child, the anointed, glorious, beautiful music that my people are going to be producing, individually and collectively, is going to be UNLIKE ANYTHING YOU HAVE HEARD BEFORE. I am only just beginning to bring about an EXPLOSION OF MY PEOPLE HARNESSING THE GIFTS AND TALENTS I HAVE GIVEN THEM TO PLAY MUSICAL INSTRUMENTS, and to play those musical instruments to worship me, to praise me and to glorify Me. Oh, my beloved child, the combination of my people playing musical instruments and singing and worshipping to me, individually and collectively, IS GOING TO BLOW PEOPLE AWAY, says I, the Sovereign Lord.

THE GIFT OF TEACHING. My beloved child, you and all my people, men, women and children, DO NOT NEED TO STUDY AT COLLEGE OR UNIVERSITY TO TEACH MY WORD, to teach my Word that is alive and active and sharper than the sharpest two-edged sword, FOR MY SPIRIT IS YOUR TEACHER. My Spirit leads into ALL TRUTH, and as my people begin living life as my hands and feet, as my disciples, as my glory carriers, the amount of LIFE-CHANGING TEACHING THAT IS GOING TO BE DELIVERED to other people is beyond anything that you can comprehend.

My beloved child, I have given you a MERE GLIMPSE of how I have only just begun to flood the earth with an explosion of my chosen people, men, women and children, beginning to use, to harness, to share publicly the gifts and the talents that I have put inside of them.

Many of my people have lived holding on to their gifting, to their talents, not wanting to use it, not wanting to share it publicly, for they have feared the response and reaction, BUT I AM SETTING MY PEOPLE ON FIRE. I am SUDDENLY CONVICTING PEOPLE OF ALL AGES to begin to USE, to begin to HARNESS, to begin to SHARE the gifting that is inside of them, the talent that I have put inside of them, that which has been burning inside of them hidden.

NO MORE, says I the Sovereign Lord, will my people hold on to and keep hidden the gifts and talents that are inside of them.

My beloved child remember this. If you could speak all the languages of earth and of angels, but you didn't love others, you would only be a noisy gong or a clanging cymbal. If you had the gift of prophecy, and if you understood all of my secret plans and possessed all knowledge, and if you had such faith that you could move mountains, but you didn't love others, you would be nothing. If you gave everything that you have to the poor and even sacrificed your body, you could boast about it. But if you didn't love others, you would have gained nothing.

Love is patient and kind. Love is not jealous or boastful or proud or rude. It does not demand its own way. It is not irritable, and it keeps no record of being wronged. It does not rejoice about injustice, but rejoices whenever the truth wins out.

Love never gives up, never loses faith, is always hopeful and endures through every circumstance. Prophecy and speaking in unknown languages and special knowledge will become useless, but love will last forever. Now your knowledge is partial and incomplete, and even the gift of prophecy reveals only part of the whole picture. But when the time of perfection comes, those partial things will become useless. When you were a child, you spoke and thought and reasoned as a child. But when you grow up, you put away childish things. Now, you see things imperfectly, like puzzling reflections in a mirror. But then you will see everything with perfect clarity. All that you know now is partial and incomplete, but then you will know everything completely, just as I the Lord your God now knows you completely.

Three things will last forever - Faith, Hope and Love - and the greatest of these is love.

My beloved child, you, your brothers and sisters, and all people walking the earth whom I haven't yet given the eyes to see and ears to hear , your eyes haven't seen, your ears haven't heard and your minds haven't conceived what I the Lord your God have got planned for you and all those who love me.

I HAVE ONLY JUST GOTTEN STARTED, says I the Sovereign Lord.

February 28th 2023

I Am Bringing About A Oneness In The Spirit That No-one Walking The Earth Has Experienced Before, Says The Lord

My beloved child, you are receiving my words now, for I am sharing with you how I the Lord your God are bringing about a ONENESS IN THE SPIRIT that no-one walking the earth today has ever experienced in their lifetime.

As I am pouring my Spirit out upon my people, as I am giving my people the eyes to see and ears to hear, as I am lifting the veil, as the scales are falling from my people's eyes, as I am putting my Spirit into my people, my chosen Sons and Daughters, including you, my beloved, are beginning to experience a ONENESS IN THE SPIRIT THAT YOU HAVE NEVER EXPERIENCED BEFORE.

In MY Kingdom, it does not matter how long you have been walking with me, the Lord your God,

In MY Kingdom, it does not matter how many pieces of scripture you have memorised.

In MY Kingdom, it does not matter what age you are.

In MY kingdom, it does not matter what sins that you have committed.

In MY Kingdom, it does not matter what people have done to you.

In MY Kingdom, it does not matter what you have followed before in your life.

In MY Kingdom, titles and statuses mean absolutely nothing.

In MY Kingdom, denominations are utterly destroyed.

In MY Kingdom, you my beloved child, have been given ALL POWER AND ALL AUTHORITY OVER THE ENEMY.

What my people are beginning to experience upon the earth, is DISCERNMENT unlike they have ever had before, to discern when a message is from me, by my Spirit, and when a message is not from me, or by my Spirit.

I AM POURING WISDOM AND REVELATION into my people, and my chosen people are pouring this wisdom and revelation out into the lives of their brothers and sisters.

There is an OUTPOURING OF DIVINE REVELATION THAT I AM GIVING MY PEOPLE.

The FLOODGATES have started to open.

The TSUNAMI OF REVELATORY TRUTH HAS BEGUN, says I the Lord of lords, the King of kings, the one given the name above all names.

The reason that you are experiencing a QUICKENING INSIDE OF YOU, is that I the Lord your God say ENOUGH IS ENOUGH of you living with ANY CHAINS TO YOUR PAST.

Your FREEDOM, my people's FREEDOM, comes from me and me alone, and I AM setting the captives free. I AM setting the captives on fire. I AM pouring my Spirit out upon my people, and there is a oneness in the spirit, because my Spirit is your teacher, and my spirit, the Spirit of truth, LEADS INTO ALL TRUTH.

I the Lord of lords, the King of Kings, by my Spirit, I AM OBLITERATING EVERY SINGLE MAN-MADE DECEPTION.

I AM OBLITERATING every man-made INDOCTRINATION.

I AM SETTING MY PEOPLE FREE from the GLOBE DECEPTION.

I AM SETTING MY PEOPLE FREE from the DECEPTION OF PEOPLE EXPECTING SOME IMMINENT RAPTURE, SOME SIMULTANEOUS RAPTURE.

MY FIRE, MY DEVOURING FIRE, is falling upon my people, and I am putting my DEVOURING FIRE on the tongues of my people, so that when they speak, BLAZING COALS OF FIRE COME SHOOTING FROM THEIR MOUTH to obliterate ALL the schemes, ALL the devices, ALL powers, ALL principalities, ALL strongmen, of the kingdom of darkness, for MY KINGDOM IS AN EVERLASTING KINGDOM, and I have begun SHAKING EVERYTHING THAT CAN BE SHAKEN.

Your eyes have not seen, your ears have not heard and your mind has not yet conceived what I the Lord your God have got planned for you because you love me.

Look around at the nation's, look and be amazed, for I am doing something in your own day that you wouldn't even believe, even if someone told you about it.

Hear this, you leaders of the people. Listen, all who live in the land. In all your history, has anything like this ever happened before? Tell your children about it in the years to come, and tell your children to tell their children. Pass the story down of MY WORLDWIDE REFORMATION from generation to generation.

My beloved child, don't think in any way the people who have been committing detestable sins, the seven things that I the Lord your God detest - haughty eyes, a lying tongue, hands that kill the innocent, a heart that plots evil, feet that race to do wrong, a false witness who pours out lies, a person who sows discord in a family - DON'T THINK IN ANY WAY THEY WILL GET AWAY WITH IT.

I AM continuing to bring my WRATH AND MY JUDGEMENT UPON THE WICKED.

I AM continuing to SUDDENLY convict people of their detestable sins.

I AM continuing to SUDDENLY lift the veil and bring people to their knees.

I AM continuing to SUDDENLY tear down rulers and leaders.

I AM continuing to SUDDENLY bring my DIVINE JUSTICE into the lives of my people.

I AM continuing to SUDDENLY set each one of my people on fire with my Spirit, for them to join you in becoming a part of MY ARMY OF GLORY CARRIERS that I have been assembling since early 2020, and make no mistake about it my beloved child, I the Lord your God, I HAVE ONLY JUST BEGUN RAISING UP MY ARMY OF GLORY CARRIERS.

YOU HAVE NOT SEEN ANYTHING YET.

Keep your eyes focused on me.

Lean not on your own understanding.

My ways are higher than your ways, and my thoughts are more than anything that you can think or imagine, just as the heavens are higher than the earth.

Come to me, my beloved child, for WISDOM EVERY DAY, and I will give you wisdom. I will not rebuke you for asking, but ensure that your faith is in me the Lord your God and in me alone.

As you are receiving my words now, I am RELEASING INTO YOUR LIFE FAITH IN ME, IN MY WORD, THAT IS ABSOLUTELY PURE.

From this moment going forward, my Word is going to be coming alive in your heart, in your spirit, unlike you have EVER EXPERIENCED BEFORE.

Wisdom and revelation are going to be getting poured out into your life by my Spirit, for my GLORY, says I, the Sovereign Lord.

My will be done, on earth as it is in heaven, says I, the King of Glory.

January 20th 2022

I Am Flooding Your Dry Wastelands With My Living Waters, Says The Lord

My beloved, I have chosen you to be a prophet to the nations. I have set you apart. I have put my spirit in you and the spirit that is in you is greater than the spirit that is in the world. My hand is mighty upon you. I have anointed your head with oil. I am the miracle worker. Rivers of living waters are flowing from my belly into your life now. All the areas of your life, of your family, that were dry, barren wastelands are now being flooded with my living waters, for I, the Lord of Heaven's Armies have spoken.

I reached down to the bottom of the deepest, darkest oceans to rescue you. I have lifted you out of the miry clay and I have put your feet on the solid rock, the rock of all ages. You are fearfully and wonderfully made in my image. I am the mighty warrior that saves. I have broken every chain of bondage in your life, because of sins and iniquities through your family generational bloodline. I have redeemed you, I have cleansed you of your sins and I am pouring out My Spirit upon you now.

I the Lord your God have not given you a spirit of fear, but of power, of love and over sound mind. From this moment forward, you will walk by faith and not by sight. You will trust in me and in me alone. You will devour by word. Your faith comes by hearing and hearing by my words. I am pouring into you now wisdom like you have never had before, discernment like you have never had before, faith that you have never had before, patience like you have never had before. Forgiveness is in your heart now. You have a heart of forgiveness for I the Lord your God has spoken. And you now can pray with all your heart, with a pure heart, with clean hands, you can pray for those who have come against you, and you can pray for their deliverance and you can pray for me to move in their life and I will move in their life because you have got clean, pure hands cleansed by my blood.

You mine, your family members are mine, you are so precious in my eyes. I formed you, I created you, I knitted you together in utter seclusion in the dark of the womb. I knew you before you were born. I chose you before I created the Heaven's and the earth. I have seen every single thing that you have ever been through. I have seen your pains, your grief, your turmoil. I have seen every single one of your tears. Yes, every single one of your tears, and I have captured them in my bottle. And you, my beloved, you have sown with tears and you are going to reap with joy for I the Lord your God, the Lord of Heaven's armies has spoken.

What have been the dry bones in your life, what has been dead and buried in your life, and the dry bones that have even become powder because of how dead they have been dead. The dry bones are going to come alive. For I the Lord your God has spoken. I am the miracle worker. I am the way maker. What has seemed impossible in your life is possible with me. I have heard your prayers. I am going to answer your prayers. I am the miracle worker. You are going to be seeing your loved ones that have turned away from you, they are going to turn and come back to you for I the Lord your God have spoken.

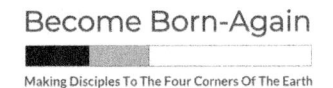

I am going to be giving people dreams, visions and nightmares to awaken them out of their sin, to awaken them out of their darkness into my glorious light, for I the Lord of Heaven's armies has spoken. You my beloved are going to be shedding tears of joy as I move in your life like I have never moved before. I am only just getting started in your life. I do not put new wine into old wineskins because old wine skins, your old self, would not be able to handle my new wine. The new wine would spill but no, I the Lord your God have been refining you by fire, but like Shadrach, Meshach and Abednego you have not been burnt up because I the Lord your God had been in the refiner's fire with you. You are mine. My hand is mighty upon you, and I have been preparing you refining you for this time right now. 2022 is going to be a glorious year for you my beloved. Victory is coming, breakthrough is coming, provision is coming. The spiritually dead are going to be coming to life, all for my glory in my name. The dry bones are going to be rattling and coming alive. There is going to be tissue and skin and muscles put on to the dry bones and then you will be prophesying into these dry bones, saying dry bones come alive. May the winds of my breath from the north, the south, the east and the west you will be prophesying into the dry bones and the dry bones will come alive. Yes, you and your family. You are going to be an army coming alive in me, the Lord of Heaven's army. I am the resurrection and the life. I am the King of kings. I am the Lord of lords, I am the name above all names, above cancer, above diabetes, above every single mental health affliction that has ever been given to anyone in your family life.

I am roaring, the chains are breaking, the curses, the strongmen have been destroyed in my name. I am roaring, I am the chain breaker, I am the King of glory and you are my precious beloved servants. You are so precious in my eyes. So, so precious. Greater is the spirit that is in you than the spirit that is in the world. You resist the devil and he flees from you. You put on the full armour of God so that you can take a stand against the devils schemes. I have made a table for you in the presence of your enemies, but Satan is under your feet. You now know that I work in ALL things for God because you love me and you live according to my purpose for you, and my ways are perfect. My ways are perfect. My ways are perfect and I now give you my peace. My Peace is a gift the world cannot give you. Peace be still. Peace, be still. Peace, be still. Peace, be still.

March 23rd 2023

The Harvest Is Waiting For You To Plant Seeds & Water Seeds Every Single Day, Says The Lord

My beloved, I desire to give you wisdom and understanding about the HARVEST.

My Word tells you to look around, for the harvest is ready.

My beloved child, I have called you by name from your mother's womb to be one of my disciples.

I have called you to be my HANDS AND FEET.

I have chosen you to be one of my GLORY CARRIERS.

As you live your life day to day, from this moment going forward, I the Lord your God are going to be giving you opportunities to be the one I have chosen to meet people at the EXACT, PRECISE, MOMENT OF NEED.

In your day to day activities, when you see other people - activities which could be deemed to be mundane or not significant - I am going to be giving you opportunities to share my love, to share the Good News, with people that you see.

It could be that the person that you see has no idea that I love them, that I surrendered my life on the cross to save their life.

It could be that that person is at that moment, when you go over to them, they are feeling helpless, they are feeling hopeless, and they feel that their life is not worth living. You will be the one that I will use to SUDDENLY reveal to them that they are not only loved by me, but that I have chosen them, that yes they like you are CHOSEN AND NOT FORSAKEN.

Another person that my Spirit will be convicting you to go and speak to, they have been asking inside of them "Is God real?", "Is there something out there?", "What is the purpose to life?", and my beloved child, you will be the one to SUDDENLY share with them the revelation that I am real, that I am the creator of all things, and that I have chosen them to LIVE IN FREEDOM.

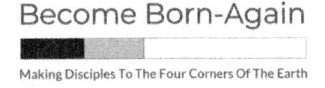

Other people I will be sending you into the life of, are my followers who have fallen away because they have been going through trials and tribulations, but you will be the one that I will use to SUDDENLY make them comprehend that I the Lord your God work in ALL THINGS IN THEIR LIFE FOR GOOD, that I am for them and not against them.

Other people that I am going to be sending you into the life of, will have prayed to me before I then send you into their life. YOU WILL AN ANSWER TO PRAYER.

Through their encounter with you, I will give them the eyes to see and the ears to hear, for you my beloved child, you are filled with my Spirit and you carry my Spirit and my presence with you WHEREVER YOU GO.

My beloved child, I am imploring you now to comprehend that THE HARVEST IS TRULY READY.

In your day to day life experiences, I desire for you to EMBRACE ENCOUNTER AFTER ENCOUNTER AFTER ENCOUNTER of my chosen people who need to hear about me, about my love, THROUGH YOU, FOR YOU ARE MY HANDS AND FEET.

You are my messenger my beloved child, and may you NEVER, EVER UNDERESTIMATE THE IMPACT that your words can have on someone else's life.

I have put my Spirit into you, and greater is the Spirit that is in you than the spirit that is in the world.

My beloved child, no longer hide your light under a bushel IN ANY WAY.

SHINE BRIGHTLY FOR ME.

My beloved child, the more that you do to advance my Kingdom, the more people that you are willing to speak to about me, the more that you are focusing your heart and your mind on advancing my Kingdom - my promise to you is the more that you will see me moving in your life and in your life circumstances in ways in which you cannot even imagine.

My beloved child, share my message to your brothers and your sisters.

The harvest is truly ready, and the harvest is waiting for you my beloved child to PLANT SEEDS AND WATER SEEDS EVERY SINGLE DAY, says I the Sovereign Lord.

May 24th 2022

Saturate Yourself With My Kingdom, And I Will Saturate You With My Glory, Says The Lord

My beloved, you are my masterpiece. I have called you by name to be my glory carrier. You are fearfully and wonderfully made in my image. You can do all things through me who gives you strength. Your identity is in me and in me alone. Before I created the Heavens and the earth, every day of your life was written in my book, every single moment, including this moment right now, was laid out before a single day had passed.

My beloved, you know my Words, that your faith comes by hearing and hearing by my Word. You know my Word that tells you, my beloved, you do not live by bread alone, but by every Word that comes from my mouth, and my beloved, you know, that I have called you to worship me in spirit and in truth. I am calling you now to truly pick up your cross, and follow me. I am calling you, my beloved, to saturate your entire being each day with me, with my Word, following what I am calling you to do each day.

My beloved, as I am pouring into you now my Spirit, as I am opening your heart more than ever before, to receive more and more of my goodness, of my unfailing love, of my grace, of my peace, of my wisdom, now, my beloved, is the time for you to saturate your eye gates and your ear gates with the things of my Kingdom.

Every day, my beloved, spend time alone with me.

When you wake up in the morning, seek my Kingdom and my righteousness first, and ALL else will be given unto you. Surrender to me each morning.

Call out to me.

Ask me to lead you and guide you through every single moment of the day ahead. When you are at home, when you are in the car, when you are living life each day, listen to anointed worship music.

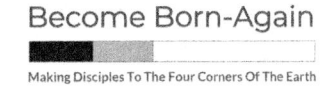

Be in fellowship with me more and more and more each day.

Completely switch off from worldly events from worldly news.

Continue spending more and more and more of your time with your brothers and sisters.

My beloved, you will have experienced in this last two years, in relationships that you once had, I have been closing doors that no man can shut. I have been closing doors on relationships that no longer serve you, with where I am taking you at this moment. But I the Lord your God, I have also been opening doors that no man can shut. I have been opening doors to relationships with your brothers, with your sisters, which are incredibly important. I have been building you up. I have been bringing more and more wisdom into your life, through the Kingdom connections that I have brought about, that I have orchestrated in your life.

My beloved, the more that you saturate your life each day with the things of my Kingdom, with my Word, listening to worship music, seeking me, speaking to me, thanking me, asking me to lead you and guide you, asking me for my wisdom, hearing my voice and doing what I am calling you to do, the more that you saturate your life with me and the things of my Kingdom, the more and more and more of my glory you will be experiencing, because I am at the King of glory.

Your eyes, my beloved, have not seen, your ears have not heard and your mind has not yet conceived what I the Lord your God have got planned for you because you love me. The more that you surrender to me, the more that you let go of all inhibitions, the more that you seek me, the more that you serve me, the more and more and more glory that will be coming into your life. You will be going from glory to glory to glory. You will be brought into floods of tears, as I suddenly bring breakthroughs into your life, as I suddenly bring about that what you have been praying for, as I suddenly bring about the transformation.

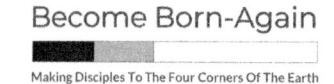

Be prepared, my beloved. Be prepared for me to saturate your life with my glory as you saturate each and every one of your days with me with my Kingdom, following my will, and through your deepening relationship with me, with your eyes, you will see more and more of my beauty in my Creation. You will marvel more and more and more at my miracle Creation. So, your life, will become more and more glorious, more and more beautiful and you will truly be stepping into the calling that I have placed upon your life, for you, my beloved, to be my glory carrier, says I the Lord of Heaven's Armies.

February 13th 2023

YOU Are Going To Be Experiencing My Glory Cloud, Says The Lord

My beloved child, you are receiving my message to you now, for I want you to truly know that your eyes haven't seen, your ears haven't heard and your mind hasn't yet conceived what I have got planned for you, because you love me.

What you have personally experienced, of my Spirit, of my glory, is NOTHING AND I REPEAT NOTHING to what you are going to be experiencing of MY GLORY.

You may well have seen and become aware of what I have been doing at Asbury, but my beloved child, I the Lord of lords, the King of Glory, I AM ONLY JUST BEGINNING POURING OUT MY SPIRIT UPON ALL FLESH.

My promise to you, my beloved child, is that YOU are going to be experiencing for yourself, MY GLORY CLOUD. The WIND of MY GLORY sweeping through where you are going to be, both on your own individually and when you are with your brothers and sisters, and you are not just going to experience my glory once.

Your life my beloved child is going to be GOING FROM GLORY TO GLORY TO GLORY.

IN MY TIME, my beloved child, you will see that you will no longer look at how I have been pouring my glory out in different areas across the entire stationary earth that I created, but YOU TOO will be a part of EXPERIENCING and WITNESSING MY GLORY coming upon a gathering of my people, of my chosen people.

Oh my beloved, precious, fearfully and wonderfully made child, I have called YOU by name from your mother's womb to be ONE OF MY GLORY CARRIERS, TO BE MY HANDS AND FEET.

I have put MY FIRE UPON YOUR TONGUE, so my beloved child as you move forward more than ever before, there are going to be BLAZING COALS OF FIRE SHOOTING FROM YOUR TONGUE as you speak my Word, as you declare my Word, as you decree my Word.

Oh my beloved child, MY GLORY, MY POWER, MY PRESENCE, MY MIRACLE HEALING POWERS, have only just begun falling upon the earth.

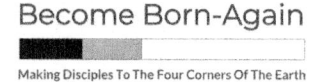

You and your brothers and sisters across the earth HAVE NOT SEEN ANYTHING YET.

I AM THE KING OF GLORY, and my glory is now just beginning to flood the earth like a TSUNAMI, like an AVALANCHE - MY GLORY CLOUD, says I the King of glory.

April 22nd 2023

I Am Making Myself & My Kingdom ABSOLUTELY IRRESISTIBLE, Says The Lord

My beloved child, you are receiving my words now, for I the Lord your God desire to give you a greater understanding, a greater comprehension, a greater revelation of how I the King of glory are rescuing lost people who have lived their whole life not believing in me, not trusting in me, having not surrendered their life to me.

I have put my Spirit into you. I have put my Spirit into a number of men, women and children currently walking the earth that is a number that you cannot comprehend, and every moment of every day I am putting my Spirit into more people.

My Spirit produces this kind of fruit in your life and in the lives of all my chosen people… love, joy, peace, patience, kindness, goodness, faithfulness, gentleness, and self-control. There is no law against these things.

My beloved child, through you and my people across the earth, I the Lord your God, I AM MAKING MYSELF IRRESISTIBLE FOR PEOPLE WHO HAVE NEVER BELIEVED IN ME, as I am pouring my RIVERS OF LIVING WATERS into you and my people.

My rivers of living waters are flowing from your hearts, out into the lives of the people who I am rescuing, who I am setting free, who I am giving the eyes to see in the ears to hear.

My beloved child I AM MAKING YOU IRRESISTIBLE to even the most BITTER, the most ENVIOUS, the most JEALOUS, the most PRIDEFUL people in your life, and people who I am going to be bringing you into the life of.

I AM MAKING YOU IRRESISTIBLE because it is not you that live, but I the Lord that lives in you. MY LOVE, MY AGAPE LOVE, MY UNFAILING LOVE WHICH LASTS FOREVER, IS IRRESISTIBLE.

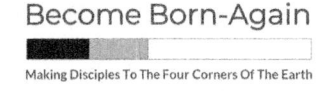

The people that I have created, that I have allowed to live their life their own way, to live in their sin, to deny me, to deny the Father. I have allowed them to be in the wilderness, to be in those chains of misery, to live battling with the things from their past. I have allowed them to live self-centredly. I have allowed them to follow man's wisdom and to not fear me, the Lord your God. I HAVE ALLOWED IT ALL.

YET NOW, three years in to me bringing in A NEW AGE, I the Lord of lords, the King of kings, the Alpha and the Omega, the beginning and the end, the First and the Last, I am making myself and my Kingdom, through my people, IRRESISTIBLE.

There is no-one that is too far gone.

There is no one living with any types of addiction that is too far gone. It is not their will that will be done, it is my will and I the Lord your God, desire for EVERYONE TO UNDERSTAND THE TRUTH AND TO BE SAVED BY MY RIGHT HAND.

As I am continuing to PURIFY my people…

As I am continuing to CLEANSE my people…

As I am continuing to SANCTIFY my people…

As I am continuing to CONSECRATE my people…

As I am continuing to make my people more and more HOLY…

As I am continuing to completely SEPARATE my people from the things of the world…

As I am continuing to draw you my beloved child CLOSER AND CLOSER to me…

I am making you, as one of my disciples, more and more and more irresistible to be around.

My promise to you, my beloved child, and share this message with your brothers and sisters too, is that I am going to be OPENING THE FLOODGATES, the floodgates of people in your life and whom I will be bringing you into the life of, WHO YOU BE PRAYING FOR, for me to set them free. When you say these five words, "Can I pray for you?", because of my irresistible, unfailing, tangible love in you, the response you are going to be getting back is "Yes please".

My beloved, I have given you a mere glimpse of how irresistible I am making myself through you and all my people to the lost people of the world, but whatever you have seen me do already in your life, however you have seen me move my beloved child, your eyes have not seen, your ears have not heard and your mind has not yet conceived what I the Lord have got prepared for you.

SMILE for I have called you by name from your mother's womb to be one of my increasing number of men, women and children who are MY IRRESISTIBLE DISCIPLES, my irresistible glory carriers, my irresistible hands and feet.

Remember, it is not you that live but I that live in you, and it is I your Lord and saviour who are making myself and my kingdom, ABSOLUTELY IRRESISTIBLE.

June 25th 2023

I Am Raising Up A People Whose ONLY Desire Is To Advance My Kingdom, Says The Lord

My beloved child, I the Lord your God, the Holy One of Israel, have chosen you to be one of my people that I am raising up, who **I am setting free from every single deception that has come through man,** by indoctrination.

I am raising up a people who are willing to **humble themselves like a little child**.

I am raising up a people who are **truly willing to let go of every single thing** that sinful, deceitful man has ever told them or talk to them.

I am raising up a people who **will not tolerate sin of any kind**.

I am raising up a people who **know that my Spirit is their teacher.**

I am raising up a people **who do not need any man to teach them what is true**, for my Spirit, the Spirit of truth, leads my chosen people into all truth.

I am raising up a people who have not been walking with me very long, yet **I have chosen them to expose the deceptions of man.**

I am raising up a people **whose pride I have crushed**, and who are willing to listen, to hear and to learn from other people.

I am raising up a people **who have pure hearts and clean hands.**

I am raising up a people who are **harnessing the gift of discerning spirits**, for **they have humbled themselves.**

I am raising up a people who will continue to **expose those who are in religion.**

I am raising up a people who **will not compromise from my Word.**

I am raising up a people who I know that **I can trust to harness and to use the gifts of my Spirit.**

I am raising up a people who **know that I have chosen to be my glory carriers.**

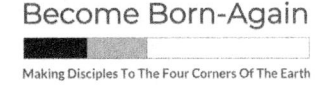

I am raising up a people **who know it is not they that live but I the Lord your God that lives in them.**

I am raising up a people who know that **the same power that raised me from the dead lives in them.**

I am raising up a people whose **only desire each day is to advance my kingdom.**

I am raising up a people who are showing me that **I can trust them with a little,** so that then **I can trust them with a lot.**

I am raising up a **people in all areas of society and at all levels of society,** to bring my Kingdom down from heaven upon the earth.

I am raising up a people **who are my hands and feet upon the earth.**

I am raising up a people who **focus on the things of heaven, not the things of earth.**

I are raising up a people **who truly know that they are going to be doing the same things that I have done and even greater things.**

I am raising up a people who **I can trust to steward Kingdom wealth.**

I am raising up a people that **I have put my words upon their tongue.**

I am raising up a people that will not allow anyone, whether a believer or not yet a believer, **to quench my Spirit that is a work within them.**

I am raising up **a people who are a part of my army... men, women and children.**

My fire, **my devouring fire, is beginning to shoot from their lips.**

My fire, my devouring fire, is upon their tongue, and my beloved child, **many are called but few are chosen.**

I have chosen you, yes you my beloved, to be one of my glory carriers.

You will **go when I ask you to go.**

You will **speak when I ask you to speak.**

You are going to be **living every day outside of your comfort zone.**

My beloved child, you can do and you will do all things in your life through me, the Lord your God, and it is not by your strength, it is not by your might, **it is by my Spirit**

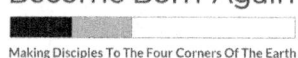

that you and all my people will live their life worthy of the calling with which they have received.

I am the King of glory, and my glory is coming into the world and across the earth out to the four corners, more and more and more.

My Kingdom come, my will be done, on earth as it is in heaven, says I the Sovereign Lord.

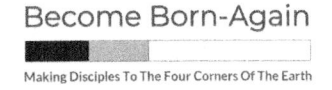

June 8th 2023

See The World & People Through My Eyes & Not Your Own Eyes, Says The Lord

My beloved child, I desire for you to experience an increasing amount of your time each day **seeing the world through my eyes and not your eyes.**

When you are seeing the world through your eyes, you can so easily be consumed with the **circumstances** of your life, the **trials** in your life, the **battles** going on in your life, the **things of earth**, things in the physical realm.

When you are seeing the world through my eyes, your experience of life begins to dramatically change.

When you are seeing the world through my eyes, you can begin to **be my hands and feet upon the earth**.

When you are seeing the world through my eyes, **you are seeing people as I see people**. I created them. I formed them. I brought them forth on the day they were born. I have put my breath into them. I have numbered every hair on their head. I know what they are going to say before they even say it. I surrendered my life on the cross for them. I shed my blood on the cross so that they can be forgiven for all their sins.

When you are seeing people through my eyes, **you begin to truly love your neighbour as yourself**.

When you are seeing people through my eyes, you are **not judging**, you are **not critiquing**, you are **not condemning**, you are **not comparing**, but you have a passion and a desire within you by my Spirit for them to come to know me.

Remember, my Word tells you freely give as you are freely received.

You have received salvation by grace through your faith in me, for **I chose you**. You didn't choose me, so you can never boast about it.

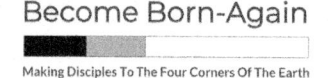

You know that everyone who calls on my name will be saved. But how can the people that you see each day in your life moving forward call on me to save them unless they believe in me? And how will they believe in me unless they know about me? And how will they know about me unless someone tells them? And how will someone go and tell them unless they are sent? That is why the Scriptures say "How beautiful are the feet of messengers who bring good news."

My beloved child, I have called you and I have chosen you to be one of my disciples. I have chosen you to be my hands and feet and you are receiving my words now, for I desire for you to experience more and more and more of your life each day moving forward, **seeing the world through my eyes and not your own, and seeing people through my eyes and not your own**.

Will you go?

Can I send you?

Are you willing to overcome your fear of man and live only with a reverent fear of me the Lord your God?

Are you truly willing to cling to me and me alone, rather than clinging to your life? For if you cling to your life you will lose it, but if you lose your life for me you will receive life.

Remember, **your purpose on earth is to be one of my disciples**, to be my hands and feet, to be one of my increasing number of men, women and children across the earth who I have called and who **I have chosen to be my glory carriers**.

May 27th 2022

Allow Me To Speak To You Each Day Through My Creation, Says The Lord

My beloved, I have called you by name. You are chosen by me and not forsaken. Before I created the Heavens and the earth, every day of your life was written out, every single moment of your entire life that has ever been, that is taking place right now as you are hearing my words, and every single moment to come in your life, was laid out before a single day had passed. My plans for your life and your family, are plans for good and not for disaster, to give you a future and a hope.

My beloved, during the last two years, I have been revealing to you that you cannot trust in man. I have been showing you that you need to put your trust and your faith in me and in me alone, in order to be able to understand and to comprehend and to navigate through day-to-day, what has been going on in your life.

Yes, I have been shaking everything that can be shaken in your life. Yes, I the Lord your God have sent the locusts out into your life, and those locusts have been stripping you down and stripping away from you all your old habits, behaviours, thought patterns and belief systems from you living in the fallen world, in which you were born into on the day I brought you forth. I have allowed you and all my people to experience deception, to experience indoctrination, to be lied to, to be manipulated, to live their life thinking they don't need me. My people have been living their life self-centeredly, living in sin, but everything that has been done in dark is being brought to light. I am exposing sin. I am exposing deception. I am exposing corruption. My worldwide reformation and revival has only just begun, and my message to you now my beloved is to open your heart truly to me. Be willing to pick up your cross and follow me. Be willing to follow me. Be willing to be hated by the world. Be willing to be my glory carry, because I have called you by name to be my glory carrier, and from you receiving my words to you now, from this moment forward as you are living in my creation, as each day you are seeing and often experiencing different weather, my beloved, I want to speak to you through the weather that you will be experiencing in your life moving forward.

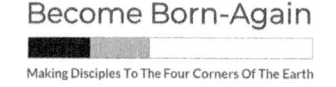

My beloved, when the sun is shining and visible, my beloved see this as I am shining my glory into your life, because you are my glory carrier. See the sun shining upon you is that I am replenishing you, I am filling you with my spirit, with my glory. I am shining down upon you because you are my masterpiece, says I the Lord of Heaven's Armies.

When the clouds come, when the sun is behind the clouds, my beloved before rain may come, but when you see clouds as you look up to the sky, see this is me speaking to you and inviting you to just come into my presence, for a period of calm, a period of peace, a period of rest, a period of contemplation, a period of you reading my Word, worshipping me, hearing from me. My beloved, I want you to feel my presence, I want to feel that I am speaking to you each and every day, because I am, and I am giving you the eyes to see how I want you to experience my Creation.

When the rain starts coming down my beloved, I want this for you to signify that I am flowing into you rivers of living waters. I am cleansing you. I am purifying you. I am pouring into you my living waters, because through your faith in me and in me alone, rivers of living waters will be flowing from you through your belly. You have been called my beloved to be my glory carrier, so now from this moment forward, when the rain starts coming down, rather than that having any form of negative effect on what you think what you feel, see it was my rivers of living waters pouring into your life, and not just your life but into the lives of your brothers and your sisters. Because my beloved remember this, every man, woman and child walking the earth, their life, their experiences, what they think, what they feel, what they believe, whether they have given me their life yet or not, every single day and every moment of their life was laid out before a single day had passed. Everyone upon the earth, as I am saying these words to you now, is precisely and perfectly where I planned them to be before I created the heavens and the earth.

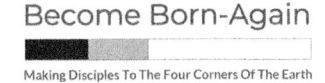

You are living through my worldwide reformation and revival, says I the King of glory, and my beloved, when you see thunder and when you see lightning I see this as a reminder to you that I am reminding you and I am reminding my people that I am the King of glory, that through your reverent fear of me, this is the beginning of all wisdom. The storms, the lightning bolts, this is me displaying that I am Sovereign, that I am in control and that I am sending storms into the lives of people who are living in sin, because of their disobedience to me, because of their denial of me, because of them living for themselves, the storms are coming into their life, the locusts have been sent into their life, they are going through the furnace, they are in the furnace, and I am doing things in the lives of people that you love that you would not even imagine.

People may plan all kinds of things but my will is going to be done, says I the Lord of Heaven's Armies, and my beloved when I send wind, as you experience wind, see this that I am sweeping away from you any recent sins, I am sweeping away from you the things that are a part of your flesh, of your old wineskins. I am sweeping away the things that are not from me, leaving you living in your new wineskins so that I can continue to pour into you my new wine, my new glory, my new provisions, my new breakthroughs, my new miracles coming into your life.

My beloved, your eyes haven't seen, your ears haven't heard and your mind hasn't conceived what I the Lord your God have got planned for you because you love me, and now as my Creation comes alive for you, as I speak through the different weather that you will be experiencing from this moment on for the rest of your life, know that I'm speaking to you, that I am either cleansing you, purifying you, bringing the wind of change running through, keeping you in reverent fear of me, shining my glory upon you, and pouring into you rivers of living waters.

I am for you and not against you. My hand is mighty upon your life. You are my beloved, the apple of my eye. Praise me, worship me, worship me in spirit and in truth. Saturate yourself with my Word. In my Word, in worship, cut yourself away from the things of the world. Be my glory carrier.

Speak about me more and more and more, and the more that you speak of me, the less you will speak of yourself.

The more that you speak of me, the more breakthroughs will be coming into your life.

The more that you speak of me, the more that you will feel my presence.

The more that you speak about me, the more that you will feel my peace.

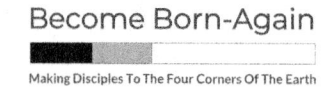

The more that you speak about me the more glory and glory and glory will be coming into your life, because you my beloved, I have called you by name to be my glory carrier, to go from glory to glory to glory, says I the King of Glory.

April 20th 2023

Hear Me Saying To You "I Created It ALL, I Sustain ALL Life", Says The Lord

My beloved, I desire for you to truly MARVEL and be in AWE AND WONDER AT MY CREATION throughout every single day of your life moving forward.

I the Lord your God, the One who created you, the One who knitted you together in utter seclusion in the depth of your mother's womb, the One who brought you forth on the day you were born, the One who has numbered every hair on your head, the One who knows what you are going to say even before you say it, the One who is for you and not against you… I the Lord your God are going to be SPEAKING TO YOU ABOUT MY CREATION THROUGH EVERY SINGLE DAY OF YOUR LIFE.

When you look at SOMEONE, I will say to you "I created them. Every day of their life is written in my book. Every moment of their entire life was laid out before a single day had passed. I sustain their existence. I love them".

When you look at a TREE, I will say to you "I CREATED that tree. I know EVERYTHING about that tree. I know precisely when that tree first started to grow out of the ground."

When you look at a FLOWER, I will say to you "Look at the beauty of my creation! Look at the intricacies of this flower that I created! Marvel at THE IMMEASURABLE NUMBER OF DIFFERENT FLOWERS THAT I THE LORD HAVE CREATED".

When you look at a VEHICLE, I will say to you "Look and marvel at that which I have created through the hands of people that I have created, using their brains that I have created! Consider every single component of that vehicle that I have created, that I KNOW EVERYTHING ABOUT."

When you look up to the SKY during the day, marvel at the BEAUTY, at the MAJESTY, the UNIQUE CLOUD FORMATIONS on that particular day.

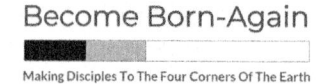

When you glance at the SUN, the great light that I created that I placed in the firmament to rule the day, smile as you comprehend that I am the King of glory, and as you are looking at the sun, I will say to you "My beloved child, MY GLORY IS SHINING UPON YOU."

As you look up to the BLUE SKY, I will say to you "Look at the WATERS THAT ARE ABOVE THE FIRMAMENT."

SMILE as I am speaking to you through every single day of your life.

As you see AEROPLANES flying in the sky, I will say to you "Look at that which I created. Look how I sustain it in the air. I know everything about that aeroplane. I have numbered the hairs on the head of every single person on that aeroplane. Every single moment of the pilots life was laid out before a single day had passed. I know precisely the speed that that aeroplane is flying out."

My beloved child, as you look at your own hands I will say to you "I created you. You are my masterpiece. You are fearfully and wonderfully made in my image. I have put my Spirit into you, and grater is the Spirit that is in you than the spirit that is in the world. It is not you that live but I that live in you. Your hands, my hands, your hands are healing hands."

My beloved child, as you see a LITTLE BABY OR A LITTLE CHILD SMILING, see that this is me smiling to you. I will say to you "Look at my precious little child that I created."

When you see BIRDS flying in the air, I will say to you "I wrote in my book for your life for your eyes to be seeing that bird flying in the sky right now. I created that bird. I sustain that bird. I know how many feathers there is on that bird. I know when that bird is next going to eat. I see everything that that bird is seeing as it flies in the sky."

My beloved child, EVERYWHERE that your eyes look throughout each day, I will be speaking to you and I will be saying to you "I CREATED IT ALL! I SUSTAIN LIFE!"

You are my precious child. You are the apple of my eye. You are my masterpiece.

My beloved child, SMILE, for I the Lord your God are smiling upon you now, and I will always be smiling upon you.

Your help comes from me the Lord, the Creator of the heavens of the earth, the Creator of all things, and I am proud of you, my beloved child.

February 3rd 2023

I Speak Directly & Personally To You Through My Creation, Says The Lord

My beloved, you are receiving my message to you now for I the Lord your God desire that during each day of your life, you see with your eyes that I am speaking to you directly and personally THROUGH MY CREATION.

Remember, I CREATED ALL THINGS.

You are led by my Spirit. Where you look with your eyes is led by my Spirit. Every day of your life is written in my book. Every single moment was laid out before a single day passed. When your eyes suddenly look to some words, immediately by my Spirit you will see that I am speaking to you through those words.

The words could be on ANYTHING that you see with your eyes.

You are going to be smiling, my beloved, for by my Spirit I will be saying to you "See how I am speaking to you through my creation?!"

Your experience of life in me the Lord your God, from you receiving my message here, is going to become more GLORIOUS, more PROFOUND, and more MIRACULOUS.

You are going to truly begin to comprehend of how significant and how important you are to me.

My beloved child, you are my masterpiece. You are the apple of my eye. I made you in my image.

The more that you experience through every day glimpses of my Glory, the more that you will be desiring to live your life worthy of the calling that you have received, and that is, my beloved child, TO BE MY GLORY CARRIER.

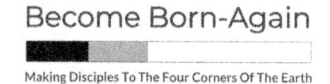

I have already done mighty mighty things in your life. You have already seen my hand in your life. You already know about my grace, my mercy and my unfailing love. You have already had the revelation of what I did for you on the cross, but my beloved, fearfully and wonderfully made child, my promise to you now is that your eyes have not seen, your ears have not heard and your mind has not yet conceived what I the Lord your God have got planned for you because you love me.

Talk about me and my miracle working powers and my signs and wonders more and more, and talk about yourself less.

It is not you that live but I that live in you.

February 2nd 2023

I Am Going To Be Using Numbers To Show That I Am Continually With You, Says The Lord

My beloved child, during your life there have been particular numbers that you have seen, that have given you a particular thought, feeling or emotion.

As you are receiving my message to you now, I am giving you the eyes to see and the ears to hear, that as you move forward, from this moment, more than ever before, I am going to be using NUMBERS in your life. NUMBERS that you will see in your day to day life to show you that I am continually with you, and that every day not only am I speaking to you by my Spirit, not only am I speaking to you through my Word, not only am I speaking to you through some of the people in your life, whom I will give you discernment that they are speaking for me, I am also going to be using NUMBERS.

When you see particular NUMBERS, know that it is I the Lord your God that are showing you that number, for my Spirit has led your eyes to see that number, for you to smile knowing that there is a scripture related to that number.

When my Spirit leads your eyes to see the number 77, immediately think of Matthew 7:7 - "Ask and you will receive, seek and you will find, knock and the door will be open to you".

When my Spirit leads your eyes to see the number 333, immediately think of Jeremiah 33:3 - "Ask me and I will tell you remarkable secrets you do not know about things to come".

When my Spirit leads your eyes to see the number 444, immediately think of Isaiah 44:4 - "They will thrive like watered grass, like willows on a riverbank".

When my Spirit leads your eyes to see the number 2222, immediately think of Isaiah 22:22 - "I will give him the key to the house of David, the highest position in the royal court. When he opens doors no one will be able to close them. When he closes doors no one will be able to open them".

When my Spirit leads your eyes to see the number 666, immediately think of Psalm 66:6 - "He made a dry path through the Red Sea and His people went across on foot. There we rejoiced in him".

When my Spirit leads your eyes to see the number 107, immediately think of Psalm 107:1 - "Give thanks to the Lord for He is good. His faithful love endures forever" and verse two "Has the Lord redeemed you? Then speak out! Tell others He has redeemed you from your enemies" and verse three - "For He has gathered the exiles from many lands, from east and west, from north and south".

When my Spirit leads your eyes to see the number 1111, 11 11, immediately think of Isaiah 11:11 - "In that day the Lord will reach out his hand a second time to bring back the remnant of His people. Those who remain in Assyria and northern Egypt, in southern Egypt, Ethiopia and Elam; in Babylonia, Hamath and all the distant coastlands".

My beloved child, I am always aiming for you to know that I AM IN ALL ASPECTS OF YOUR LIFE, EVERY MOMENT, EVERY SECOND OF YOUR ENTIRE LIFE, for remember, I knew you before you were conceived. EVERY DAY of your life is written in my book. EVERY MOMENTS was laid out before a single day had passed.

Your life, from receiving this message now, is going to increase in the glory, in my glory, that you're experiencing EVERY DAY.

Embrace ALL the experiences I'm giving you.

Come close to me and I will come close to you.

Remember, my Word tells you in Romans 8:28, "I WORK IN ALL THINGS FOR GOOD for you because you love me, and because you live according to my purpose for you".

Thank you my beloved child for receiving my message now.

My will be done, on earth as it is in heaven, says I the Sovereign Lord.

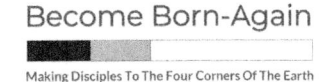

October 12th 2022

Every Time You Experience Rain I Want You To Smile, Says The Lord

My beloved, every time you experience rain from receiving my message to you now, I want you to smile. I want you to see that as the rain is coming down, I am cleansing you, I am washing you, I am purifying you, I am refreshing you.

My beloved, when the rain starts to come down, whether light or heavy, see it that I am pouring into you rivers of living waters.

No longer have your spirit dampened when I send the rain.

No longer have your mood dampened by the rain. Instead, my beloved, may you have a happiness, a joy and a peace about you as the rain comes down.

Embrace the rain.

My beloved, my promise to you as you take hold of my message here, that as you move forward in your life in me the Lord your God, at different moments in your life when you are having a significant experience, when you are doing my work, when you are being my hands and feet, at different moments of your life where there is a significance to what is taking place, at times you will see that I will bring the rain, and I will immediately speak to you and say "My beloved, I told you I am bringing rivers of living waters into your life and into the lives of those people around you and the lives of people that you are with, when you are doing my work, and I bring the rain".

Embrace when the rain comes.

Embrace when the showers come.

Embrace when heavy rain comes.

It is all from my hand, and it is me pouring my rivers of living waters into your life, so that rivers of living waters flow from your heart, for your faith is in me and in me alone, says I the Sovereign Lord.

September 11th 2022

You Are Not Going To Enter Into Another Season, Says The Lord

My beloved, you have been through many seasons in your life. As you reflect back on your life, both before I saved you and set you free, before I lifted you out of the miry clay, your life before you came into relationship with me, and your life since coming into a relationship with me, your life has been a series of seasons.

You have had challenging seasons.

You have had happy seasons.

You have had breakthrough seasons.

You have had peaceful seasons.

You have had stormy seasons.

You have had seasons in your life, which have almost broken you.

You have had times in your life when you felt like you were never going to break through, you were never going to break free, you are never going to experience love, joy, peace in ways in which you have longed to experience love, joy and peace.

You have had season after season after season.

My beloved, you not going to enter into another season. You are now about to enter into life in me, as my GLORY CARRIER. I have been preparing you, through your entire life and during the last few years and the last few months, to receive my message to you now. You are not entering into a breakthrough season. You are not entering into a season where your prayers will be answered. No longer think that you will have good seasons, bad seasons and seasons in between.

My beloved, you are beginning to truly understand that I work in ALL THINGS FOR GOOD because you love me and because you live according to my purpose for you. You are going to be living each day in joy and peace. Joy overflowing.

You are going to be worshipping me, thanking me and praising me EACH DAY. No weapons formed against you will EVER PROSPER, and every tongue that rises up against you, you will condemn, for that is the heritage of the servants of me, the Lord your God.

You are going to be flying like an eagle above the things below.

No longer will you be affected by the things taking place in your life like you used to be.

No longer will your flesh take over.

No longer will you be battling with feelings and emotions when things take place in your life, because each day my beloved, as you walk by faith, not by sight, as you seek my Kingdom or my righteousness first each day, all else will be given unto you, and you are going to be filled each day with my Spirit, so you will be experiencing life IN ME filled with my Spirit, seeing your life through my eyes, because my way is perfect.

You will no longer be grumbling, you will no longer be complaining, you will no longer be frustrated, you will no longer be asking the question why? You will be worshipping me, you will be praising me, you will be thanking me, you will be glorifying me, you will be talking about me, you will be testifying about me, you will be saturating your eye gates and your ear gates and from your tongue will be you talking about me each and every day, for the more that you talk about me the less that you talk about yourself.

The seasons of your life have come to an end. You are now about to embark on the rest of your life as being my glory carrier, and my promise to you my beloved, the more that you desire me, the more that you hunger for me, the more that you fix your eyes on me, my beloved, I am going to be taking you from glory to glory to glory to glory, for I am the King of glory, and you my beloved, precious, fearfully and wonderfully made servant, you are my glory carrier, says I, the Sovereign Lord.

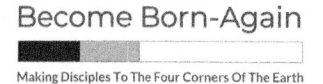

October 11th 2022

My Promise To You Is That You Are Going To Be Rich Beyond Your Wildest Imagination, Says The Lord

My beloved, I the Lord are going to make you rich beyond your wildest imagination.

You haven't lived your life being rich, but my promise to you is that as you desire every single day to be in a deepening, intimate relationship with me the Lord your God, that you are going to become and stay rich.

My beloved you are going to be rich in my peace which surpasses all understanding, which guards your heart and your mind.

My beloved you are going to be rich in my blessings, which I am going to be pouring into your life, more and more and more.

My beloved you are going to be rich in experiencing my unfailing love for you, every single day.

My beloved you are going to be rich in experiencing my glory in your life.

My beloved you are going to be rich in miracles, signs and wonders, for I am now giving you truly the eyes to see, the ears to hear and the heart of flesh to comprehend that I have called you by name to be my glory carrier.

My beloved you are going to be rich in my joy, says I, the Sovereign Lord.

My beloved you are going to be rich in the fruits of this Spirit.

My beloved, you are going to be rich in my rivers of living waters that I am flowing into your life right now, and they are going to be flowing from your heart for your trust and your faith is in me, the Lord your God, and in me alone.

My beloved, my promise to you is that you are going to be rich beyond your wildest imagination, and your family members, your friends and all those who I will be bringing into your life for the rest of your life will also see that you are rich.

I have been preparing my storehouses in heaven to pour into your life. The more that you talk by faith and not by sight, the more that you glorify me, the more that you talk about me and less about yourself, the more that you testify of my goodness, the more that you are my hands and feet, the more of my riches I'm going to be pouring into your life, says I the Sovereign Lord.

June 29th 2023

Are You Honouring Me With Your Wealth? Asks The Lord

My beloved child, my Word tells you to **honour me with your wealth.**

My Word tells you that **it is a sin to know what you ought to do** and then not do it.

My Word tells you to **freely give,** as you have freely received.

My Word tells you that **if you are lukewarm, neither cold nor hot,** I will vomit you out of my mouth.

My beloved child, you know that everything that you have is because of me, that I am your Jehovah Jireh.

You know that every good gift and every perfect gift comes down from me.

The money that you have in your bank is my money.

My question to you, my beloved child, is **how would you feel if I asked you to share your bank statement publicly?**

How does it make you feel **if other people were to see what you spend your money on,** and how much money you spend in your day to day life?

My beloved child, are you honouring me with your wealth?

Are you living your life having denied yourself and where you pick up your cross daily to follow me?

When you spend money, is it sometimes for **selfish reasons,** for your **own pleasure,** for your **own entertainment,** for your **own needs,** or when you spend money, are you spending money knowing that you are my hands and feet, knowing that I have chosen you to be one of my disciples?

My beloved child, are you honouring me with your wealth?

Each day, **are you living your life worthy of the calling that you have received,** and that is to be one of my disciples?

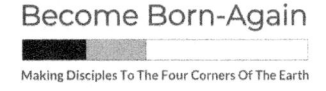

My Word tells you to not be ashamed of the Gospel for it is the power of God that brings salvation to all who believe.

My Word tells you to **freely give as you have freely received.**

My beloved child, as you are receiving my words now, as I continue to purify you, as I continue to sanctify you, as I continue to refine you, remembering that **only those with pure hearts and clean hands can climb my holy mountain,** my beloved child, if today you wouldn't be comfortable in sharing your bank statement publicly, **I am taking you to a place where you live your life each day, where you would be comfortable sharing your bank statement publicly.**

Remember my beloved child, **to honour me with your wealth, to freely give as you have freely received, to let your light shine before others, to live your life without any fear of man** and instead live only with the reverent fear of the me the Lord your God.

My beloved child, it will be futile for you to fight against my will.

You may plan all kinds of things, but my will is going to be done.

I am taking you to a new place of purification, of sanctification, for my Word tells you that you are to be Holy, just as I am Holy, says I the Sovereign Lord.

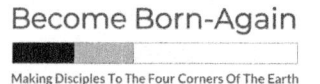

September 23rd 2022

For The Rest Of Your Life In Me, Talk By Faith, Not By Sight, Says The Lord

My beloved, you know that my Word calls you to walk by faith and not by sight.

My beloved, I am now calling you, for the rest of your life in me, to talk by faith, not by sight.

Talk to other people about the promises that I have given you that you are standing on.

Talk to other people about the things that are impossible with man that are possible with me, the Lord your God.

SPEAK LIFE into what appears to be dead and buried.

Declare and decree my Word.

Prophesy into the dry bones in your entire family lives circumstances.

My beloved, with all your heart, with complete belief and trust, TALK BY FAITH. Share your faith in the things that I haven't YET done in your life.

My beloved, my promise to you, through your total surrender to me, through you making me the Lord over your ENTIRE LIFE, my Word tells you that you can pray for anything, and if you have faith, you will receive it. So my beloved, through your faith in me and in me alone, my promise to you is that your loved ones whom I haven't YET lifted the veil, I haven't YET removed the scales from their eyes, I haven't YET given the eyes to see and the ears to hear, I haven't YET softened their hardened hearts, my promise to you my beloved, through your absolute total faith, and through you talking by faith, my promise to you is that IN MY PERFECT TIME, I will set the captives free in your life.

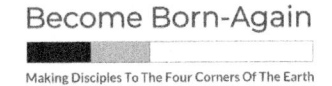

So my beloved, as you are receiving my words to you now, by my Spirit, you can truly begin to not just walk by faith, but you can TALK BY FAITH. You can be willing to sound crazy. You can be willing to sound what some may describe as delusional, but remember my beloved, when you send my Word out, it does not return to me void, it accomplishes all that I desire and it prospers EVERYWHERE that I send it.

Matthew 21:22 tells you my beloved, that you can pray for anything, and because you have faith, YOU WILL RECEIVE IT.

Continue to talk by faith.

Continue to talk about the salvation of your loved ones that hasn't YET happened.

Continue to talk about the miracles that haven't YET happened in your life.

Continue to talk by faith and not by sight.

My beloved, your eyes have not seen, your ears have not heard and your mind has not yet conceived what I the Lord your God have got planned for you because you love me.

My beloved, my time has not YET come to bring about the miracle salvations of your loved ones, of the things that you have been praying for, MY TIME HAS NOT YET COME, BUT MY TIME IS PERFECT, AND MY TIME WILL COME, says I the Sovereign Lord.

April 30th 2022

Get Ready To Hear Me Say "I Told You I Would Do It", Says the Lord

My beloved Sons and Daughters, this is the Lord your God. My message to you now is that in my perfect time, all my promises to you will come to pass and when they do you will hear me say to you "I told you I would do it" and you will be weeping. You will be weeping tears of joy.

The things that are on your heart right now, as I speak these words, your greatest desires of your heart that haven't yet been fulfilled, that haven't yet come to pass, including those which seem truly impossible. In my perfect time, you will see that all my promises to you are yes and Amen. I will fulfil the words and the promises that I have spoken to you, because when I send my word out, it does not return to me void, it accomplishes all that I desire and it prospers everywhere that I send it.

Your eyes haven't seen, your ears haven't heard and your minds haven't conceived what I the Lord your God have got planned for you because you love me.

Be prepared my beloved Sons and Daughters, for me to say to you, "My beloved, I told you I would do it. My beloved, I told you, you would see family reconciliation. My beloved, I told you that you would see the breakthrough. Oh, my beloved, I told you I would heal you. My beloved, I told you, you can trust in me.

July 24th 2023

Each Day You Will Know My Voice, Hear My Voice & Trust My Voice, Says The Lord

My beloved child, many are called but few are chosen. **I the Lord your God have chosen you.**

My hand is mighty upon you. I have anointed your head with oil.

My Word tells you, "Come close to me and I will come close to you."

My beloved child, I am calling you to desire each morning when you wake to **first of all, seek my Kingdom and my righteousness and all else will be given on to you.** When you wake in the morning, before you get on with your day as my hands and feet, come to me and say "Lord today, not my will be done, but Your will."

My beloved child, fix your eyes on me. I am the author and the finisher of your faith. Your help comes from me, the Lord your God, the Creator of the heavens and the earth. **I created all things. I sustain all things.** It is my breath in your lungs. I am for you and not against you, and if I am for you, who can ever be against you?

The battle that you have each day, the battle that rages, is between your flesh and my Spirit, and you have your sin nature, **and it is impossible for you to overcome the dictates of your sin nature without my Spirit, without you desiring to speak to me, to listen to me speak to you, to read my Word, to hear my Word, to listen to worship music.**

Oh my beloved child, I have plans for your life and plans for your family, **plans for good and not for disaster to give you a future and a hope. I have chosen you to be FORERUNNER in your generation, to be a TRAILBLAZER in your generation.**

My beloved child, I have put my Spirit into you, and greater is the spirit that is in you than the spirit that is in the world. **You can do ALL THINGS through me, the Lord your God who gives you strength.**

I am putting my words upon your tongue.

I have placed a hunger and a desire inside of you to saturate your **eyegates** and your **eargates** with the things of my Kingdom, because **my Word is truth, my Spirit is the spirit of truth, and I AM the Way, the Truth and the Life** and no-one can come to the Father except through me.

My beloved child, as you are receiving my words to you now, I am pouring my Spirit into you. I have been giving you **spiritual eyes to see.** I have been giving you **spiritual ears to hear.**

I am beginning to give you greater and **greater revelation of my love for you.**

I surrendered my life on the cross to save your life. Yes to save your life. I shed my blood on that cross to be the atoning sacrifice for all your sins.

I have chosen you, you haven't chosen me.

Before I created the heavens and the earth, I planned out, I wrote in my book this very moment, the seconds that you are hearing my words to you.

You are mine.

You are FREE in me the Lord your God.

You are no longer a slave to fear.

You are no longer a slave to your sin nature.

You are no longer a slave to your flesh.

It is the power of my Spirit at work within you that is going to **lead and guide and direct you throughout each and every day.**

My beloved child, as you are receiving my words now, **I am giving you the gift of discerning of spirits.** Each day, throughout each day, you will **know my voice.** You will **hear my voice.** You will **trust my voice,** because of my Spirit within you. Yes, you will know that I am continually speaking to you, and as you read my Word, as you hear my Word, **I am going to be giving you wisdom and revelation of who you are in me,** of how significant you are to me and for my kingdom.

I am going to be using you mightily. YES I am going to be using you mightily.

Each day ask me, "Lord, use me today. How would you like to use me today?" and when I answer, be willing to go. **Be willing to be obedient and I will bless you for your obedience.** Yes, blessing upon blessing upon blessing for your obedience.

I have chosen you to be my hands and feet upon the earth.

Each day as you wake up, as you leave your home, know that you are walking the earth as one of my disciples. **Know that you are my hands and feet and the same power that raised me from the dead lives in you!**

Thank you, my beloved children, for receiving my words to you now.

The peace that I give you is a gift the world cannot give you. My peace, which surpasses all your understanding, guards your hearts and your minds in me the Lord your God, the Holy One of Israel, the Sovereign Lord, the Alpha and the Omega, the great I AM.

July 19th 2023

Increase Your Levels of Expectation, Says The Lord

My beloved child, you are receiving my message here for **I desire for you to raise your levels of expectation of you seeing and experiencing my glory**, to greater and greater heights.

Since early 2020, so often without you even realising it, **I have been separating you out from the things of the world.** I have been giving you the eyes to see and the ears to hear what my Spirit is saying.

You have lived your life in your flesh, walking in your flesh, often battling with your flesh with feelings and emotions that are not from my Spirit.

I have been **purifying** you.

I have been **cleansing** you.

I have been **sanctifying** you.

I have been **consecrating** you.

I have been giving you **wisdom and revelation** through my Word, which is alive and active.

I have been **teaching you my ways.**

I have been **convicting you of the sins** that you have been committing.

My Spirit has brought you to a place of repentance.

You have been learning to put your faith in me the Lord your God, and in me alone.

Since early 2020, you have seen demonstrations of my glory.

You have watched some of my Sons and Daughters being used by me to demonstrate the miraculous, to demonstrate my miracle working powers, to bring my glory down from heaven upon the earth.

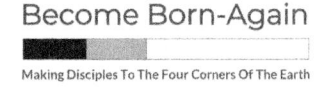

Through everything that you have been experiencing in your life personally and through what you have seen me do through some of my Sons and Daughters across the earth, without you realising it, **I have been raising up your expectation levels** for you to see, for you to witness, for you to experience my glory in ways in which you have never experienced before.

My beloved child, many are called but few are chosen. I have chosen **you** to be one of my disciples. Yes, I have chosen **you** to be my hands and feet. It is not you that live but I the Lord that live in you, and you can do and you will do all things through me the Lord your God who gives you strength.

I have put my Spirit into you, and you know that there are 9 gifts of my Spirit.

As you are receiving my message here for the first time, there are only some of the gifts of my Spirit that you have been experiencing, that you have been witnessing, but when I send my Word out into your life, it does not return to me void, it accomplishes all that I desire and it prospers **everywhere** that I send it, and my message to you now, my beloved child, is that as you increase your level of expectancy for you personally to experience my glory, you will see that you will be harnessing more of the 9 gifts of my Spirit.

Oh my beloved child, your eyes have not seen, your ears have not heard and your mind has not yet conceived what I the Lord your God have got planned for you because you love me.

My promise to you is that you are personally going to be seeing and experiencing my glory manifest in your life and in the lives of people around you, more and more and more.

Increase your expectancy my beloved child.

I am the miracle worker, and **what is impossible with man is possible with me** the King of kings, the Lord of lords, the King of Glory.

Yes, I am the King of Glory, and I have chosen you to be one of my glory carriers.

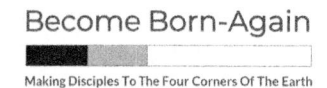

Increase your expectancy my beloved child, for **you have not seen anything yet, and no-one walking the earth today has ever witnessed** what they are going to be witnessing over the coming days, weeks, months and years, **as I continue to once again shake the heavens and the earth.**

My Kingdom come, my will be done, on earth as it is in heaven, says I the King of glory.

July 23rd 2023

My Chosen Generation Is YOUR Generation, Says The Lord

My beloved child, you are receiving my message now, for I desire to **give you wisdom and revelation about which generation in the world today** have I chosen to be THE generation that is going to **bring my glory down from heaven upon the Earth** more than any other generation that has gone before.

My beloved child, my chosen generation is YOUR GENERATION.

Yes, that is right, my beloved, fearfully and wonderfully made servant, **it is your generation that is a chosen generation, for I have called you, I have chosen you, to be my glory carrier.**

It does NOT matter **what age you are.**

It does NOT matter **what you have done during your life.**

It does NOT matter **how long it has been since I gave you the eyes to see and ears to hear.**

It does NOT matter **how much of my Word you have read.**

It does NOT matter **whether you have denied me for the entirety of your life,** and it is only NOW that I am lifting the veil. It is only NOW where the scales are falling from your eyes.

Oh my beloved child, my hand is mighty upon you!

Many are called but few are chosen, and **you my beloved child are a part of my chosen generation.** For I have called and I have chosen and I will continue to lift out to the darkness, men and women of ALL ages, teenagers, children of ALL AGES ages, they are ALL MY CHILDREN, I CREATED THEM ALL!

It is my breath in their lungs!

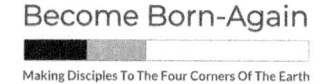

Become Born-Again

Making Disciples To The Four Corners Of The Earth

My beloved child, share this message with your brothers, with your sisters, with your family members.

For your generation, their generation, is my chosen generation, and my Kingdom come, my will be done, on earth as it is in heaven.

I am pouring my Spirit out upon all flesh. Men, women, teenagers and children, no matter their circumstances, no matter their life, no matter whether they have known me or not during their life, I AM pouring my Spirit out upon them. I am using them as my hands and feet.

More and more men, women and children are beginning to harness and to use the 9 gifts of my Spirit.

The gift of faith.

The gift of prophecy.

The gift of words of wisdom.

The gift of words of knowledge.

The gift of praying in tongues,

The gift of interpreting tongues.

The gift of the working of miracles.

The gift of healing.

The gift of discerning of spirits.

I have only just begun giving my people the eyes to see and the ears to hear.

I have only just begun rescuing my lost sheep.

I have only just begun bringing my people out of Egypt.

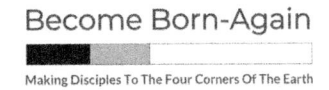

I have only just begun lifting my people out to the miry clay.

I have only just begun destroying the addictions that have been killing my people.

I have only just begun bringing in a new age.

I have only just begun once again shaking their heavens of the earth, for **what is happening now has happened before, and what will happen in the future has happened before because I the Lord your God make the same things happen over and over again.**

Look around at the nations! Look and be amazed, for I am doing something in your own day, **something that you wouldn't even believe even if someone told you about it.**

Oh my beloved child, **share my message.**

Everyone alive today is living in my chosen generation, for I have called all my people to come home.

I want everyone to be saved and to understand the truth, and when I send my Word out, it does not return to me void. It accomplishes all that I desire, and it prospers everywhere that I send it.

EVERY GENERATION is my chosen generation, says I the King of Glory.

This Year Is Going To Be The Most Life Changing Year Of Your Entire Life, Says The Lord

My beloved, this year is going to be THE MOST LIFE CHANGING year of your entire life so far.

My desire for you is for you to come into a more DEEPER and more INTIMATE PERSONAL RELATIONSHIP with me. I am IMPLORING you, my beloved child, to truly desire to love me with all your heart, all your mind, all your soul and all your strength.

My beloved, be truly willing to completely separate yourself from worldly things.

Be truly willing to LET GO OF EVERYTHING that deceitful, sinful man has taught you during your life.

Become like a little child, and let me the Lord your God be your teacher in ALL THINGS.

My beloved, seek my Kingdom and my righteousness first every morning, and my promise to you is that all else will be given onto you.

Read and listen to my Word more than you ever have done before, and listen to other people reading my Word less and less and less.

FOCUS on me and my Kingdom, not on earthly things. Remember, I am Sovereign. I am in control. Everything and everyone is in precisely and perfectly the place that I planned them to be before I created the heavens and the earth.

My beloved child, you know that my Word tells you to walk by faith, not by sight. I am now encouraging you also to TALK BY FAITH not by sight. Remember, what is impossible with man is possible with me, the Lord your God.

My beloved child, this year and beyond, SATURATE your eye gates and your ear gates with my Kingdom, my Word and worship music.

DON'T LOOK BACK at former things. Don't look left or right. Instead, FIX YOUR EYES ON ME, the author and the finisher of your faith.

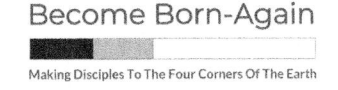

My beloved child, TRUST that you are hearing my voice during and throughout each day.

GO when I ask you to go.

Be willing to share the Gospel to complete strangers AT ALL TIMES. No matter where you may be, no matter your circumstances, there are opportunities at all times to shine light into people's darkness.

Remember my beloved child, DO NOT HIDE YOUR LIGHT UNDER A BUSHEL.

Offer to pray for people you have only just met.

Offer to pray for people for me to do a miracle heart transplant in them, taking out of them their heart of stone and replacing it with a tender, responsive heart of flesh.

My beloved child, be willing to live your life outside your comfort zone this year and beyond.

Be willing to go through new doors I will be opening up in your life.

Be thankful in ALL CIRCUMSTANCES.

Testify of my goodness more and more and more.

Don't keep praying for the same things over and over. I heard you the first time. Trust me that I have heard your prayers and I will answer all prayers that are in line with my will, IN MY PERFECT TIME.

My beloved child, accept that I truly do work in ALL THINGS for your good because you love me and because you live according to my purpose for you.

SURRENDER everything and everyone in your life to me. Let go and let me do what only I can do.

DON'T GET OFFENDED BY ANYONE. Bless those who come against you. Pray for those who persecute you.

Truly, truly, love your neighbour as yourself.

Clothe yourself in love that comes from me by the Holy Spirit.

Worship me in spirit and in truth more than you ever have.

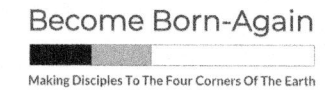

Watch your tongue. Be completely VIGILANT in what comes from your mouth.

TALK ABOUT ME MORE, talk about yourself less, and my beloved child, every day through all circumstances, give God ALL the glory, praise and honour.

July 26th 2023

You Are Going To Be Carrying My Power, My Presence & My Glory Wherever You Go, Says The Lord

My beloved child, **I have chosen you.**

I have chosen you to be my glory carrier.

I have chosen you to be my hands and feet.

I have put my Spirit into you, and greater is the spirit that is in you than the spirit that is in the world.

It is not you that live but I the Lord that live in you, and **my HEALING POWER, the HEALING POWER of my Spirit, is upon you, is within you, and my HEALING POWER is going to be going forth WHEREVER you go.**

Wherever you step foot each day, from this moment going forward, when you **speak** my Word, when you **declare** my Word, when you **decree** my Word - my Word is going to go forth. My Word is going to shoot forth.

My Word is **life**.

My Word is **healing**.

My Word **brings deliverance**, so when you send my Word out it will not return to me void. **It will accomplish ALL that I desire and it will prosper EVERYWHERE that I send it.**

My beloved child, **one of the gifts of my Spirit is words of knowledge,** and I the Lord your God, my promise to you, **through your humility, through humbling yourself, through you surrendering and dying to yourself each and every day, through having the humility of a little child,** my promise to you is that by my Spirit, **I am going to be giving you words of knowledge** about people you have never spoken to before, people you have never met before.

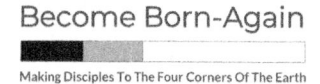

I will reveal to you "What is it about them?"

What is it about their life?

What is it about their health?

What is it about their circumstances that I want to heal, that I want to deliver them from, that I want to set them free from?

I will be giving you words of knowledge, so you can go over to them, wherever you go in your day to day life, when you see people - it can be out **in public**, it can be **at the hospital,** it can be when you **go to the shop,** it can be **anywhere where you see people** - I the Lord your God I am going to give you words of knowledge and you can then go over to that person, you can reveal to that person what I have revealed to you, what they are currently battling with.

They will know that this is a divine encounter with a child of God.

They will be in awe and wonder, and then you will be able to say to them, **"God wants to deliver you". "God wants to heal you." "God wants to set you free", and you will see people being DELIVERED AND SET FREE.**

You will see people being delivered from the spirit of WITCHCRAFT, from the spirit of RELIGION, from the spirit of UNBELIEF, from the spirit of FEAR.

You are going to see people set free and delivered, says I the Sovereign Lord.

My words are upon your lips. **I have put my words within you, and you are going to speak my Word with POWER, WITH AUTHORITY,** because I have given you ALL authority to trample over lions and cobras, to crush fierce lions and serpents under your feet.

The weapons that you fight with are not of the world. They are not carnal, on the contrary, **they have divine power to break down strongholds.**

My beloved child, I have chosen you. **I have chosen YOU to be my GLORY CARRIER,** for you to experience my glory, my power, my deliverance, my love, my healing powers, my miracle healing powers.

YOU HAVE HEALING HANDS.

When you lay your hands on people's eyes, people who have had degraded eyesight for however long, when you offer to pray for them, when you tell them **"Jesus wants to heal your eyesight. Jesus wants to give you 2020 vision"** and **when they have the faith to believe,** you will lay your hands upon their eyes and you will ask me to bring a miracle healing to their eyes, and **I AM going to restore their eyes. I AM going to give them 2020 vision. I AM going to give them new eyes.**

When you lay hands on other parts of people's bodies, where they have **ailments**, where they have **sicknesses**, where they have **disease**, where they have **muscle problems**, where they have **joint problems**, when they have **arthritis**, when they have **cancer**, when they have **any form of sickness or disease, my healing power is going to go forth from you, from your hands.**

My healing power is going to go forth and **they are going to experience a miracle healing from me, and they are going to see the glory.** They are going to see my glory, for I AM the King of glory, and you my beloved child, you are my glory carrier, and **YOU CAN DO ALL THINGS THROUGH ME** the Lord who gives you strength.

It is not you that live but I the Lord that lives in you.

Thank you my beloved child. Thank you my precious, beloved child, for receiving my words. Thank you for receiving my words. I have been pouring my Spirit into you. Yes, I have been giving you the eyes to see and the ears to hear and for you to comprehend, **THAT YOU ARE MY GLORY CARRIER, THAT YOU ARE CARRYING MY POWER, MY PRESENCE, MY SPIRIT WHEREVER YOU GO, FOR THE REST OF YOUR LIFE.**

I AM the King of glory, and you my beloved child, are going to be seeing your life go from GLORY TO GLORY TO GLORY TO GLORY, says I the King of Glory.

A Life-Changing Career Opportunity

Overview

This life-changing career is available to **anyone** who desires to live each day with **true purpose**. You will be joining an increasing amount of men, women and children in countries across the entire stationery earth who have started this career, particularly since early 2020.

This is the most rewarding career you could ever have upon the earth, and once you begin this career, **your life will never be the same**.

This career will see your relationships change as you find yourself spending more time with people with the same passion and desire and life purpose as yourself.

You will need to **make sacrifices to fulfil your potential** with your new career, but with every sacrifice you will find **your life becomes more joyful and glorious**.

Summary

- **Location** - where you live
- **Starting** - immediately
- **Hours** - from whenever you leave your home, flat, apartment, hut or caravan, to when you return to your place of rest
- **Qualifications required** - none
- **Work experience required** - the life you've led
- **Salary** - divinely provided

Essential Attributes

- Humility
- Integrity
- Passion
- Positivity
- Open-mindedness
- Love for all people
- Forgiveness of others

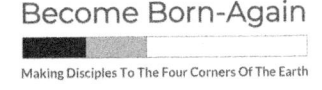

Unwanted Characteristics

- Pride
- Jealousy
- Envy
- Fear
- Self-centeredness

Who You Can Expect To Meet

- People from all walks of life
- People who are going through or who have been through what you have been through in your life
- People who have been on the verge of suicide
- People who are struggling with their mental health
- People who have lost loved ones
- People who are feeling helpless and hopeless
- People who tell you they are not religious
- People who tell you they are atheist
- People who were brought up in religious families
- People who are spiritual
- People who have never before met a disciple of Jesus
- Brothers and sisters in Christ
- Christians living in sin

What You Can Expect To Experience

- Having long, deep conversations with people you've only just met
- Witnessing people you have only just met being brought to tears as you share with them truths they didn't realise
- Having your offer to pray for people you've only just met warmly accepted
- Seeing people miraculously healed through your prayers
- A small handful of people trying to put you down with slurs and insults and false accusations, to which you will always respond in love with a blessing
- Your life going from **glory to glory to glory**

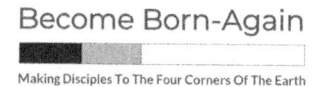

Application Process

There isn't an application process for you to go through in order for you to begin this career immediately today.

How To Start Your New Career

1. Read **God's purpose for your life** - https://www.becomebornagain.com/your-purpose
2. Read through some of the **messages to you personally, from the Lord**, on the following pages
3. Download & print some of **disciple handouts** - https://www.becomebornagain.com/downloads
4. Watch the **12 part teaching** titled "**Evangelism is Essential**" - https://www.becomebornagain.com/wisdom-testimonies/evangelism-is-essential-12-part-teaching
5. Start speaking to complete strangers by saying "**Hi, God bless you! Do you know that Jesus loves you?**"
6. **Trust that the Holy Spirit** will give you the right words to say in your divinely appointed encounters each day
7. **Keep praising and thanking God** that He has called you and chosen you to be a disciple of Jesus

"My thoughts are nothing like your thoughts," says the LORD. "And my ways are far beyond anything you could imagine. For just as the heavens are higher than the earth, so my ways are higher than your ways and my thoughts higher than

your thoughts."

Isaiah 55:8-9

And we know that God causes everything to work together for the good of those who love God and are called according to his purpose for them. For God knew his people in advance, and he chose them to become like his Son, so that his Son would be the firstborn among many brothers and sisters.

Romans 8:28-29

And I am convinced that nothing can ever separate us from God's love. Neither death nor life, neither angels nor demons, neither our fears for today nor our worries about tomorrow—not even the powers of hell can separate us from God's love. No power in the sky above or in the earth below—indeed, nothing in all creation will ever be able to separate us from the love of God that is revealed in Christ Jesus our Lord.

Romans 8:38-39

June 30th 2023

Become Born-Again Is Very Different To Almost All Other Ministries I Have Birthed In The Last 50 Years, Says The Lord

My beloved child, I the Lord your God have chosen you to receive this message about my ministry Become Born-Again.

Become Born-Again ministry is very different to almost all other ministries that I have birthed during the last 50 years.

The purpose of this ministry is absolutely focused on **making disciples to the four corners of the earth.**

At the very heart of the Become Born-Again ministry is my heart.

My Agape Love is at the very heart of this ministry.

In March 2021, out of nowhere, by my Spirit, the Become Born-Again ministry was birthed.

I have entrusted my loyal servant, Paul, to steward my ministry.

Become Born-Again ministry is not about Paul.

I will never allow my servant Paul to be lifted up, to be exalted, to be put on any pedestal at all.

I have started to use Paul and I will continue to use my servant Paul to be **a demonstration of what it means to be my hands and feet upon the earth.**

I will continue to use Paul to show you, to show your brothers and sisters, to show my people who I will bring to Become Born-Again ministry, I will continue to use Paul as **an example of what it means to deny yourself, to pick up your cross daily and follow me.**

I will continue to use Paul to demonstrate what it means to be one of my glory carriers.

I have already revealed that I have chosen **my servants Ben and Mugisha in Rwanda, and my servant Mwima in Uganda,** to be my hands and feet for my ministry Become Born-Again in their countries.

I the Lord your God are going to **continue choosing servants in more and more and more countries across the earth** to be my lead ambassador for Become Born-Again in their country.

I have only just begun expanding the reach of my messages, which I give through my servant Paul, to more and more countries across the flat, stationary Earth that I created.

There is already and they will continue to be **absolute humility at the very heart of the Become Born-Again ministry.**

There is already and there will continue to be **a purity and an integrity of the Become Born-Again ministry.**

I will not allow ANY selfish ambition in my ministry.

I will not allow ANY pride to start influencing my ministry.

I will not allow ANY jealousy or envy in my ministry.

I will not allow ANY unnecessary spending of my financial provisions in the Become Born-Again ministry.

There is already and there will continue to be **a transparency about my ministry Become Born-Again,** which my people across the earth have not seen before with other ministries.

My Spirit has already led some of my people to be cheerful givers to the Become Born-Again ministry.

Time and time and time again, I have shown my servant Paul that **I am the ministries Jehovah Jireh,** that I am faithful to my Word, that **my timing is always perfect,** that my servant Paul can have his faith in me and in me alone.

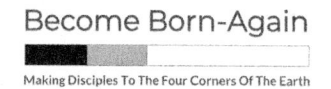

My servant Paul knows that his life on earth and the things that he does each day are to **please me and not to please man.**

My servant Paul knows that **I will continue to convict him when he is committing sin of any kind,** and that I will also ask him to **confess publicly that which I have convicted him of,** so that I the Lord your God can bring conviction on more and more of my people for those same sins.

My beloved child, my people who I will use to bless my ministry Become Born-Again, will find that by blessing this ministry, **they experience me moving in their life in ways in which they haven't experienced** when they have blessed other ministries.

I am doing a new thing with the Become Born-Again ministry.

As **I am continuing to once again shake the heavens and the earth,** the Become Born-Again ministry is one of the many intrinsic parts of I the King of Glory, the Alpha and the Omega, the beginning and the end, **bringing in a new age.**

My chosen people who are already apart of my ministry, and all my chosen people who I will be connecting to my ministry Become Born-Again, are just like the Apostle Paul, **walking, living and breathing demonstrations of what it means to be one of my disciples.**

My beloved child, look around at the nation's. **Look and be amazed, for I am doing something in your own day,** something you wouldn't even believe even if someone told you about it.

I the Lord your God are going to continue speaking through my servant Paul to give message after message after message to my people.

As time moves forward, **there will be more and more messages for people of all ages across the entire earth.**

My promise is that **I will continue to use my servant Paul to speak messages to people individually. These people will be at ALL different levels of society, across ALL areas of society.**

No-one - no man or woman - is outside of my reach.

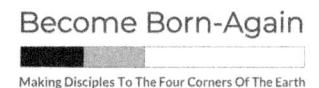

When I the Lord your God send my Word out, as I have sent my Word out here, it does not return to me void. It accomplishes all that I desire, and it prospers everywhere that I send it, and people, **yes including people in ALL the high places, they may plan all kinds of things, but my will is going to be done.**

My beloved child, **I have chosen you** to be one of my disciples.

I have chosen you to be my hands and feet.

I have chosen you to be one of my glory carriers.

Not by your strength, not by your might, but by my Spirit, **you are going to live your life worthy of the calling that you have received.**

As you continue to humble yourself as a little child, my promise to you my beloved child, is that I am going to take you from glory to glory to glory, for it is not you that live but I the Lord that lives in you, and I AM the King of glory, and my Kingdom come, my will be done, on earth as it is in heaven, says I, the Sovereign Lord.

Support The Ministry

We give God ALL the glory for everything He is doing with His ministry Become Born-Again across the earth, and we pray a blessing over all our brothers and sisters who have ever supported the ministry.

If you would like to support the ministry, knowing that 100% of any donation will pay towards day to day ministry expenses countries including England, Rwanda, Uganda, Kenya, America and Pakistan, you can do so in one of these 3 ways:

1) Make a secure online offering - https://www.becomebornagain.com/offering

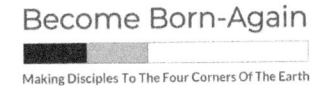

2) Make a secure offering via CashApp - https://cash.app/%C2%A3BecomeBornAgain

3) Make a secure offering via PayPal - https://www.paypal.me/becomebornagain

To everyone who has supported the ministry so far, thank you, and may God continue to bless you and draw you closer to Him each day.

Agape, Paul and all the Become Born-Again team

www.becomebornagain.com

I have told you these things so that you will be filled with my joy. Yes, your joy will overflow!

John 15:11

You will show me the way of life, granting me the joy of your presence and the pleasures of living with you forever.

Psalms 16:11

Those who plant in tears
will harvest with shouts of joy.

Psalms 126:5

I pray that God, the source of hope, will fill you completely with joy and peace because you trust in him. Then you will overflow with confident hope through the power of the Holy Spirit.

Romans 15:13

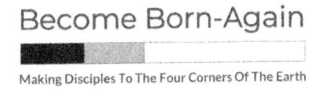

Therefore I, a prisoner for serving the Lord, beg you to lead a life worthy of your calling, for you have been called by God.

Ephesians 4:1

To download FREE PDF versions of all the ministry books, on topics including mental health, suicide, sexual abuse, becoming a disciple, the globe deception & intimacy with Jesus, go to the Become Born-again ministry website:

www.becomebornagain.com

Printed in Great Britain
by Amazon